God Has Not Forgotten You

Gloria H. Michael

BK
ROYSTON
Publishing

BK Royston Publishing
P. O. Box 4321
Jeffersonville, IN 47131
502-802-5385
http://www.bkroystonpublishing.com
bkroystonpublishing@gmail.com

© Copyright – 2017

Cover Design: Bill Lacy

ISBN-10: 1-946111-27-9
ISBN-13: 978-1-946111-27-2

Printed in the United States of America

Dedication

This book is dedicated to reminding, reassuring, and strengthening those of us who thought, and some who still think that God has forgotten us.

I pray that this book will be a source of inspiration to you, especially when things seem impossible.

Gloria H. Michael

Table of Contents

Chapter 1

Sometimes in life, we tend to think that there is no way out of our situation. Life has thrown us a curve ball, but I am living witness to the fact that although life's road seems so dark and lonely, our breakthrough is just ahead of us. Matthew 28:20 reminds us of God's presence that is always with us, *"Lo, I am with you always, even unto the end of the world."*

I have experienced God working in my life time and time again. So many times, as the last flicker of light was about to fade, God just stepped in right on time. I have had many situations in life; some good, some unpleasant, some I would not want to live through again, but they have all been learning experiences for me.

I am the second of three children born to a pastor and his wife. It is a real blessing to be born into this type of family and environment, because it saved me from a lot of things that could have befallen me. When we were children, we could not understand or appreciate why our lives were so restricted. We felt like we were always in a glass bowl for everyone to see; always having to measure up to other's high expectations.

My parents were very hard working people. My father pastored a church, and my mother was always right there by his side. The first church that my father pastored was in the district of his birth; in the island of Jamaica, West Indies where he was fondly known as Brother John. At the age of seventeen, my father taught Sunday School Class in the church where his family attended. After years of delving in the word of God in a more intent way, he decided to become more active in the church of his choice. He was ordained as an elder in this church.

My father loved the land and all its potential. He was a farmer growing different types of crops.

The types of crops grown by my father were a variety of sweet potatoes, yams and bananas. His produce helped to feed the family. He was so blessed, that many times he could help others in need. He also reared cows for supplying fresh milk, mules for transportation, chickens, ducks and pigs for meat.

I was blessed to have known both of my grandmothers on my mother and father's side of the family. Unfortunately, I did not get the opportunity to know both of my grandfathers on my mother and father's side, because they had passed away before I was born. My maternal grandmother had a large family of eight children. Being widowed never stopped her. She was also an entrepreneur. I was a very small child, but there are things that are indelibly written in my mind. Things I would never forget. She was of the Anglican faith. But because of her debilitating health problem, she was not able to attend church. She was a very quiet and petite person. Her family was also blessed to live off the resources of the land. They had limestone rocks that men would come in and dig by the barrel or truckload.

My brother and I along with my cousins lived in the neighboring district, but attended school in my grandmother's district. There were three cousins along with my brother and I that stayed with my grandmother until the weekend. Incidentally, those children are my Aunts' from my father's side of the family, and their father is the brother of my mother. I think families from small districts know how to blend in, because I have three different couples integrating on both sides of my mother and father's family.

I was the youngest of the grandchildren, and attended the preparatory school for ages four through seven. There were also other children from the district who traveled to school with us. The scenery on our way to and from school was beautiful with acres and acres of lush green trees and grass. Cows could be seen grazing in the distance. For at least two miles, there was no type of human habitation. That was not good, because we were told that there are people who were called 'black heart men' who would capture children and cut out their heart. Perhaps this was just a scary tactic to remind us of the importance of walking in groups, which we did to protect each other.

There was also a part of the road which was called 'long turn' by the people in the district. We could see our houses from a distance, but everyone had to go around the road in the form of a loop to get home. When we were given chores to complete before our parents got home, we would play most of the time until we saw our parents coming in the distance. We knew they had to go all the way around the bend, and that would give us time to hurriedly do our chores. Looking back on the things we did in our childhood years, we thought it was funny until our children devise their own strategies on us.

At the end of the school day, we both were supposed to wait until our older siblings' came to get us, and we all walk home together. One day, my friend and I decided to walk home alone; it is a day I will never forget. Everything went fine until we came to this deserted area. Out of the bushes came two young men. I could see trouble staring us in the faces. One held on to me and the other held on to my friend. My friend was cursing and trying to wrestle with him. The words that were coming from her mouth were shocking, although I was already in shock. I started to plead with the one that held on to me. I just kept repeating "please, please, please don't hurt me, don't hurt me," while my friend was cursing with the foulest language imaginable. Finally, I heard the other young man say, "let her go." Even though shock paralyzed my body and weakness filled my knees, I still found strength and took off running; not stopping until I got home. My mother was shocked to see me coming home alone. Upon arriving home, I noticed a buckle was missing from my shoe. In those days, you are fortunate to have shoes for school. And if you lost a shoe buckle, it was replaced with a safety pin. To this day, I never understood why my mother did not get upset with me. As a great mother, she may have seen that I was in enough agony. I had truly learnt my lesson.

I knew that it was the prayers of my parents, and the angels of the Lord that protected me. I grew up letting the Lord fight my battles because there is no failure in him. This incident took place in the nineteen forties. My brother hated the thought of having to walk the long distances; therefore, he would wait around to see if he could get a ride from someone. In those days, it was sometimes hours before we saw a vehicle going our way and there was no guarantee that the driver would want to give anyone a ride. That was one of the main reasons for my brother getting in trouble; he just decided he did not want to walk home. During that time, there were these big Cadillacs. The rear of the car shaped like a fish's tail. My brother called them 'fish tail Cadillac. He was constantly drawing pictures of them. Except for his work in school, I cannot remember him drawing anything other than a Cadillac. When he migrated to the United States of America, he was sure to get his very own Cadillac. He even took a picture of it and sent it for everyone to see.

We were told by my mother that her descendants were of the Maroon Indian's race. In the process of writing this book, I decided to learn more about who the Maroons were, and to get a better understanding of my ancestors.

In doing the research on the Maroons, there was a bit of difference of opinion. For instance, in one information it said that they were slaves. In another, it said contrary to popular belief, the Jamaican

Maroons were never slaves. They were referred to as a special type of people who after much struggle, fighting and eventually peace treaties, they were granted the status of autonomy. Jamaica's native inhabitants were Arawak Indians. At the beginning of the Spanish occupation of Jamaica, men were brought from Spain to be employed as security guards and tenders of cattle by the Spanish garrison. The Jamaican Maroons are descendants of Moorish men, Spanish soldiers, African men of the Ashanti guards and the Taino women. The Maroon communities waged relentless warfare against British colonialism. During the years of the war, they were forced to subsist in the mountains on wild hogs, available plants and ground provisions. Their special way of barbecuing meat has become an important way of traditional cooking. Beginning in the eighteen century, two district groups of Maroon communities emerged. The Leeward Maroons in the north and the northeast, and the Windward Maroons. This group was situated in what was called Nanny town after its leader; now known as Maroon Town. Incidentally, Nanny was said to be a fearless female fighter; a warrior. For security reasons, the Maroon villages were located in the inaccessible mountains, giving them commanding view of the lands. Guards were posted at the entrance to watch and alert the community at the approach of intruders by blowing the Abong. The Abong, is the conch shell or cow skin made into a horn as was practiced in Africa. There were times when I would see certain traits in me and my family members. It was interesting to take time out and trace our roots to find out more about ourselves.

Looking back at my mother's side of the family I can now understand the reason for their fearlessness, resilient, and determined hard working spirit. My mother was a true Maroon. She was a beautiful small woman with the strength of a mighty warrior. I remember the way she smiled, her soft curly hair and her smooth skin. She was admitted in the hospital some years before her passing. I went to see her; the nurse met me with great excitement." I thought something was wrong," she said. "I have been waiting to see someone related to her," she blurted out. This lady is in her eighties. Where are her wrinkles? She protected her children and grandchildren. She had a kind heart, but was not afraid to voice her opinion.

I was about six years old, but I can remember clearly my grandmother. She was a very kind and giving person. She would eat her dinner and leave a portion on the plate. Then she would call all five grandchildren and give each of us a piece of her food. We were taught not to eat from anyone. And even though she was our grandmother, I did not like it. I felt as if I was eating her leftovers. During those days, we did not say "no" or "I don't want it" to our elders. After becoming an adult and reflecting on these things, I can see where she was teaching us one of life's very important lesson:

'charity' which is love in action. Over the years, I can pass this giving type of spirit onto the people that are in need, including my family.

One of my fondest memories at my grandmother's home, was when she would let my uncle bring out the gramophone; otherwise known as a 'phonograph.' This tradition was done only once per year. I always wished she did it more often. It was not until years later, I realized why it was done just once per year. It was done once a year, because it was Christmas. It was a special time for playing Christmas Carols. I was so fascinated with that machine. My uncle would wind it up, put the record on and out comes that beautiful music, 'Hark the Herald Angels Sing' and other beautiful Christmas carols. On top of the gramophone was a horn with the picture of a dog on it. I would sit there mesmerized, wondering where this beautiful sound was coming from. I knew it's not from the dog on the horn, so where could it be coming from? Sitting here right now writing my story lets me reflect on how innocent a child's thinking can be.

Before long, I could sing along with words of those beautiful Christmas Carols. My brother and I went to my grandmother's church; again it was also once per year. Low and behold, they were singing the same songs that were on the gramophone. It was that one special day, 'Christmas Sunday.' I enjoyed that day, seeing the different ways of worship. And this was somewhat unusual, because the congregation was a mixed race: Black, White, English and Jamaican. As children growing up, our neighbors sometimes would give us a chicken or some type of baby animal which we would take care of, and know that we are totally responsible for rearing it. Our neighbor gave me a chicken which grew and later laid eggs; which was used specifically for hatching to have more chickens, which would be used for producing poultry and eggs for the family's consumption. She grew, laid eggs and hatched the eggs which brought forth baby chickens. She could be seen teaching her baby chicks to eat and take short walks. One day, she decided to take them on greater adventure by crossing the street; she went to the open space by our school yard. I kept a keen eye on her, since she could run into trouble with the mongoos-es or halks that will try to take her baby chicks. Lo and behold, a mongoose came along and tried to take one of her baby chick. That mother hen sprang into action to defend her babies. I stood there mesmerized at what I was seeing. She fought so hard; going for the mongoose eyes and never stopped until she plucked both eyes out. The mongoose staggered away. The mother hen went back to her chickens; they all went under her wings and like an umbrella she closed her wings. I was so shocked at what was happening. It didn't dawn on me to call my mother until I got out of this fixation that I was in. When I finally called my mother, she found the mongoose lying dead in the bushes. Except for God's love, I do not think there is any love as great than a mother's love. *Psalm 91:4 tells us that our heavenly father covers us with his feathers, and under his wings shall we trust...* We have that glorious opportunity of running under his wings in the time of trouble where we are safe and secure.

My mother was a very good cook and great at baking. One of her delights was what she called the 'Kings Pudding.' This pudding was steamed in a double boiler. That was a treat we always looked forward to eating. The big finale, was when my mother and my aunt got together to cook. They pull out all the stops. The menu would include roasted duck, stuffing and one of our national dish, rice and peas. The menu would also include something I always get excited about eating; although it makes me pucker when it hits my taste buds... shredded cabbage with only vinegar as the dressing. I would enjoy setting the table while they were cooking.

These were memorable moments of family togetherness, and I enjoyed every bit of them then and now.

My mother usually has some favorite quotes like: "Carry not tomorrow's load while there is strength to find." When I hear that, I know that if something was being worked on earlier on, we are going to finish it before the day is over. Through the years, I realized that I have become just like my mother. I've had to have everything in order. Another favorite quote, "Waste not, want not." Therefore everything that could be used, they were. The bread that is leftover is made into bread pudding or bread crumbs. The pineapple is eaten in salads, baked goods, jellies and jams. Then the skin is to make delicious drinks. The coconut is used for countless number of things; not even the shell or husk goes to waste. They are used for kindling fire or making art work. This is just an example of the ways my mother would be so resourceful and take that quote to another level.

Our home was welcoming and always open to people that were either passing through or visiting our church. On one occasion, a minister that came to preach at our assembly, got to our house about one o'clock in the morning. He was shown to his room, which was next to my brother and I's room. It was not long after our visitor retired to bed, that we heard this big bang on the floor sending shock waves through the house. My parents rushed to see what was happening. The man had fallen off the bed. He was tangled up in the sheets in such a way, that he had a hard time untangling himself to get off the floor. To this day; I am not sure how, but it was decided that some evil spirit may have entered the house with him causing that to happen. After a long wait; with our ears pricked up to hear if there would be anymore incidents, our fears subsided and we fell asleep. I kept hoping that this was his only incident before he left; thank God it was.

Another time, a young couple came to our home with their baby. They stayed for some time, maybe about two weeks. I remember a series of discussions, before them asking if the baby could stay with us for a few days. They promised to come back and get the baby. When some time passed and they did not return, my parents sent messages to them. During those days, the main form of communication was messages, telegrams or the post office. The baby's parents finally returned to get their baby with not much explanation.

Another visitor was a blind preacher, who passed through the district at least once or twice a year. He never sleeps over. He just stops by to preach, refreshes himself at our house and moves on to the neighboring town. As a child, I was very afraid of the blind. Whenever he was in the house, I would hide under the table or somewhere where I could see his feet, but I did not want to see his face. On one of his visits, I remember him saying, "I should be the one that is afraid of you, since you can see me but I can't see you."

I was also afraid of a dead corpse. In those days, there were no mortuaries in our district to accommodate the dead. The body would be kept in a designated place, or if there was space in the house, the body would be kept there until the burial. When I was about seven years old, our elderly neighbor passed away. She lived across the street from us, and I could see friends and neighbors gathering at the family's home. I asked my mother if I could go and see what was going on. No one was in the room at the time I entered it. I saw the deceased lady's foot shake under the sheet. I ran out of the room and did not stop until I reached home. If that was my imagination, it was a very strong one. Another thing that was so scary; even still in my young adult life, is to listen to the loud, low, slow chanting after someone dies. Their loved ones would have nine nights of singing. Not every family does this; it's left to the family's spiritual beliefs. I did not actually saw her face because it was covered under the sheet. But I didn't look at another dead body until approximately thirty-five years later, when I became a Christian and the Lord took all those fears away. He didn't just take my sins away; he also took away the doubt and fears replacing them with faith, courage and confidence. I could look at the members of our church that passed away withour fear. Getting over the fear of dead folks was one hurdle, but nothing could prepare me for the major loss of my closest and best friends: my husband, my mother and my father who passed away in a period of ten years. None of them showed any outward signs of illness. My mother was in her eighties, and my father was in his ninety fifth year; which I am grateful that the Lord let me see them in their golden years, but nothing could prepare me for my husband's death. It took me some time before the fact sunk in that I was a widow in my early years. When our lives are totally in the hands of the Lord and we take him at his word, he takes away our fears and replaces them with confidence. 2 Timothy 1:7 tells us that '*God hath not given us the spirit of fear; but of power; and of love and of a sound mind.*' There are times when we are challenged, tested and tired by the adversary to see if we will buckle under the stresses and fears of life, but we must reassure ourselves of God's words. His promises are true. He tells us this in Psalms 138:2, where David reminds us that God magnifies his word above His name. It is our privilege to reach out and claim them.

The setbacks in my father and our family's lives were many. Farming can be rewarding, when there is enough rain and the weather is right for crops to grow. Then on the other hand, it can be devastating when drought or storms destroy the crops. Those are times when the farmers; including my father, look at other avenues to provide for their families. An opportunity came for men to apply for farm jobs in the Unites States of America. My father was in the final group to go through that rigid test and he was successful. We were all sorry to see him go, but it was just for a period of time. The men left for the States with the promise that if they performed well they could apply again the next year. This was about the year 1944. Those U.S. dollars could go a long way to help the families; financially. They were taken to Florida where they started working on the farms.

About two weeks after they left, my brother and I; along with another group of children, were on our way home from school when we saw a truck drive pass with a group of men. Those of us whose fathers had left for the U.S. thought we were seeing our fathers; but then we wondered how could that be, since they were supposed to be hundreds and hundreds of miles away. We all started running trying to get home as fast as we could, thinking surely this was not a vision that we saw. After reaching home we found out that it was true, our fathers were back. The reason for their early return home, was that the living and working conditions were so bad that some of the men created an uproar that ended up with all the men being sent back home. Those who did not take part in the incident were not excluded from returning home. My father said they had just one night to go shopping. He bought me a very pretty hat and a doll. The doll had dark hair and brown skin that was made of a sponge-like material that caused it to feel exactly like flesh. My doll looked and felt just like a real baby. My baby and I did everything together. I even shared my food with her, which I found out was not a good idea. I woke up one morning to find, that the mouth area of my doll was chewed up by some type of rodent that must have smelled the food on her face. I was so devastated at the loss of my baby doll.

It is amazing how after digging deep into the resources of our minds, we can recall such hidden memories; some pleasant some unpleasant. Many times, I will refer to people being transported in trucks; at that time it was one of the main sources of transportation. One of my fondest memories was when my school visited the factory that made bath soap and another called the milk condensery. The truck we rode in was decked out with seats. We sang all the way to the factories and back. It was so much fun. I kept the souvenirs that we received on those trips for a very long time.

I was still attending preparatory school when we were told that there is a war going on. At that age, it did not make much sense to us. I cannot remember clearly, but I do remember the men leaving our district. I was told they were going to help England fight the war that was in progress. Often we were reminded that the war was still going on. Finally, one day while we were in school, the bells started ringing unusually all over the town. The teachers told us that the war was over and that we should go home and tell our parents. In my young mind, all that meant was, 'we get to leave school early.' When we got home, the news spread like wild fire. The men came home to fanfare and jubilee. The most important thing was that not one life was lost from the group of men that went to war from our district. A song was made for the captain and his squadron. From my recollection, the words were, 'Hurray for Captain Skervin, Hurray for Captain Skervin and his men. Captain Skervin is a soldier in the army and he never loses.'

From observation, I could see that on my father's side of the family or my paternal grandfather was very hard working, very resourceful and provided for his family. The seven siblings on my father's side of the family inherited a total of one hundred acres of farmland, in addition to a house for each sibling. There was ample land space around each house. Some of the siblings were not interested in farming on a large scale; therefore, they utilized land around their home for a family garden. My father ended up with the hundred acres of land.

My brother and I grew up hearing my father and his family calling the property Muffet. But while checking the official documents at the government office, they found that the property was registered as 'Butts Run.' On the public main road, driving or walking for about a block, one would never imagine that there is anything but hills on the other side of the property. Upon entering the property, there is level land on the other side of the hill. There were many pimento trees, avocado trees, cedar trees, mahogany trees, grass for the animals to graze, water tanks and water troughs for the animals to drink water. Some areas of that hill consisted of lime-stones. Lime-stones are rocks that are formed by accumulation of organic remains, such as shells.

I can remember watching my father making a kiln and burning the lime-stone, which comes out looking as lily white powder, which is called 'lime.' This is used to make cement and fertilizer. As a child, going around that hill with my parents, reminded me of when we are going through our mountain experiences in life. And if we fainted not, there was good waiting for us on the other side.

Bauxite was another mineral found on the property. In some areas of Jamaica, the soil has a very red color. I would describe it as dark orange red color. Research was done as far back as 1867 by an English surveyor, who noted that the red color was a mixture of iron and alumina. It was not until 1942 that attention was given to the possible economic significance of turning this red earth into bauxite for aluminum ore. American companies came to Jamaica, and began to place flags on private properties which included my father's property. As a small child, I could hear the adults saying that the flags were a sign that the Americans wanted to buy the land for mining the bauxite. Some of the people did sell their land to the American company; others including my father did not.

The entrepreneurial spirit existed on both sides of my family. My paternal grandfather grew coffee and pimento (allspice), to support his large family. I could remember during the summer months, my brother and I would help to reap the coffee beans and pimento. As a child, I thought it was a lot of fun and not a chore. Pimento was encountered by Christopher Columbus on the island of Jamaica during his second voyage to the New World. It was named by Diego Alvarez Chanca. Pimento was called allspice as early as 1621 by the English people, who thought it combined the flavor of cinnamon, nutmeg and cloves. The berries are picked when green. Traditionally dried in the sun; when dried, it resembles large brown pepper corns. The whole berries have a longer shelf life than when ground into power. They also produce ore aroma when freshly ground. It is one of the most important ingredients in Jamaica cuisine. It is also used in liqueur, deodorant, oils, spices and that famous 'jerk pork' done with the jerk seasoning and the aromatic flavor of the wood and leaves of the pimento tree. The pimento plant is dioecious and hence male plants must be kept far proximity to other fruits to allow those fruits to develop. To protect the pimento trade, the plant was guarded against export from Jamaica. Used by the Taino Indians before 1494.

I am always fascinated by how a family can sustain itself with the resources and talents that God gives us. Friends of my father's family told my mother with a giggle; that the first time her mother-in-law and father-in-law decided to take their money to the bank, they climbed into their cart with a pillowcase filled with money. Somehow I tend to believe that funny story, because they had so many children, yet could bequeath the things they had to the children.

Chapter 2

Jamaica is known for its beautiful hills, and famous Blue Mountain which rise to a height of seven thousand four hundred and two feet. It is the highest mountains in the Caribbean. The climate of this region is cool and foggy with high rain fall. The soil is rich with excellent drainage. This combination of climate and soil is excellent for the growing of coffee. And that is where we get our world class renowned excellent tasting, mild, no bitterness 'Blue Mountain Coffee.' I remember as a child, smelling the aroma from freshly brewed coffee and asking my father if I could have some. He said coffee is not for children, but he did not explain why. Those of us who are over the age of sixty knew that an explanation was not required when we were told "no you can't." Over the years I understand the expression I can't do without my cup of coffee;' therefore, I decided I don't need it. I still think that freshly brewed good quality coffee has one of the best aromas.

After reaping the coffee and pimento berries, they were taken to a 'barbeque' (a smooth open surface that is exposed to the sun), where they were placed to dry. Next they are off to the threshing, where the chaff and debris are taken out. This was the final process prior to being taken to the market for sale.

Speaking of hills, a lot of the residents must go up and down hills to get to and from their houses. It's no problem; but at a certain age with health challenges, it puts a strain on them. When my father was about ninety years of age, he was having difficulty walking up the hill close to home. I did not give much thought to the fact that he was not walking up the hill any more since he was up in age. We just thanked God that he had a reasonable portion of health and strength; a man that had only been to the doctor twice in his life. One day, the phone rang and my father was excited. He

Said, "Cutie; I walked up the hill again!"

Psalm 18:33 "He maketh my feet like hines feet." God had given him the strength to climb the physical and spiritual hills of life.

My grandmother had quite a lot of fruit and coconut trees on her property around her home. She was known to be stingy and not wanting to share. Sometimes she would let the fruits remain on the trees until the birds eat them rather than giving them away. From time to time, the children would play tricks on my grandmother to get the fruits and coconuts. My paternal grandmother said, she could not see, but I think she was not completely sightless. If someone came to pick fruits or coconuts without her permission, she would call out to them and they would take off running; having a good laugh with their goodies in hand.

The principal at our school once approached me with somewhat of a funny grin. He said, "Does your grandmother really think she is fifty-two years old?" I was about eight years old and thought that my grandmother must be older than the age she is telling the folks that she is. But it would be up to him; that if he doesn't think so, he is the right person to do the math or ask her himself.

He was a very good teacher, but had a way of putting us on the spot. For instant; my father was a very quiet and calm person. But when he sings in church, it's truly what is called making a joyful noise, not to mention when he preaches. He pulls out all the stops. On Monday morning, our principal would say to my brother and me before the entire school, "I could hear your father from a mile away; singing and preaching and all that noise. What was he thinking?" I don't know if it bothered my brother; he did not show it, but it bothered me.

I just wanted him to be quiet and leave my father alone.

Approximately sixty-two years later, I was telling my family about it and one of my daughters said, "What do you expect, the principal was just a teenager." After giving it much thought I said, "You are right." He was just nineteen years of age when he graduated from college, came straight to our school and accepted the position as principal. The most important item on our Principal's agenda was education. He often stressed how his hard work paid off. And despite his age, he greatly improved the curriculum and the general operation of the school.

My father was a very wise man and obeyed God's Word. Psalm 149:5 exhorts us to be joyful in the congregation of saints, praise His name in the dance, and let the high praises of God be in our mouth. Psalm 150 again exhorts us to praise the Lord with musical instruments. Isaiah the evangelical prophet speaking on the promulgation of the gospel in Isaiah 40 speaks of crying in the wilderness. I don't think he was talking softy. Luke 3:4 also made mention of Isaiah the prophet. If someone is excited about someone or something, they will be in other words, a 'fan' or fanatic about that person or thing.

There were times when we were in a drought season and the lack of rain caused the crops to be totally lost. But my parents just kept praying and hoping for rain. One of the hardest times I saw my parents go through was when my father invested in Jersey cows that could be milked mornings and evenings. The farmers were very excited because most of the milk was sold to the condenser in the morning, yet in the evening they still have extra milk for the family.

My father obtained a loan that was used to buy the cows for breeding and milk. The cows were costlier than the regular cows since they could give milk morning and evening. Everything went well for a while. The milk truck would pick up the milk for the condenser daily. My chore was to get the milk for breakfast, then either my brother or I would take some to the principal of our school, so that he and his family could enjoy fresh milk in the morning for breakfast.

The cows, without showing any sign of sickness, started dying. My parents were devastated. They all died except a calf. My parents tried to keep the calf alive by feeding it with a bottle to no avail. I saw my father cry for the first time, and I cannot recall having seen him cry again since. He had lost mules, ducks, cows, chickens and pigs before. But I imagine the thought of the bank loan that had to be paid; in addition to being overwhelmed with the situations, was much to swallow.

The town's people thought the number of things that were happening to my parents was odd. My parents were informed by the people about evil forces that were working against their efforts to succeed. Some folks in the district called the name of a person that was working witchcraft against my father. My father was quick to brush it aside in disbelief. He was nick named 'Job' by the town folks. Job was a man that loved God and hated evil. He has a historical personage, as evidenced by the experiences recorded in the book which bears his name. The book of Job in the Bible is a poetic book which describes his sufferings. It gives an account of the argument between himself, his friends concerning the reason for his sufferings and the solutions to his problems. In Job chapter 1:9, Satan asked God, 'Does Job serve God or nought?' To show that temporal calamities are not always the result of sin; Job a princely and wealthy man, was suddenly cast down to poverty and misery. He was forsaken and insulted by his wife and friends. But after all his disappointments, sufferings and a most severe trial of his faith and patience, he was restored to more than his former position and happiness.

Previously, I wrote about the trucks that transported both products and people. If the only bus that runs in the area was full, people would ride the truck. The wind would be very strong sometimes, and in the open back truck anything that was light and not held firmly, could eventually be blown away. My father was told about the letter that was given to a passenger on the truck to take to the Obeah man; otherwise known as the witchcraft worker, was blown away. The wind took the letter out of the messenger's hand. Someone found the letter and the news spread in the district. When my father heard, his answer was "If it is so, it may affect the things around me, but it will not harm me." As I grew older, I realize what my father meant.

It's there in Job 1:12, "And *the Lord said unto Satan, behold all that he has is in thy power; only upon himself put not forth thy hand.*"

Also, Psalms 91 says, "*He that dwelleth in the secret place of the most high shall abide under the shadow of the Almighty. I will say of the Lord, He is my refuge and my fortress; my God; in him will I trust.*

Surely he shall deliver thee from the snare of the fowler, and from the noisome pestilence.

He shall cover thee with his feathers and under his wings shall thou trust: his truth shall be thy shield and buckler.

Thou shall not be afraid for the terror by night; nor for the arrow that flieth by day.

Nor for the pestilence that walketh in darkness, nor for the destruction that wasteth at noonday.

A thousand shall fall at thy side, and ten thousand at thy right hand; but it shall not come nigh thee.

Only with thine eyes shalt thou behold and see the reward of the wicked.

Because thou hast make the Lord, which is my refuge, even the most High, thy habitation;

There shall be no evil befall thee, neither shall any plague come nigh thy dwelling.

For he shall give his angels charge over thee, to keep thee in all thy ways.

They shall bear thee up in their hands, lest thou dash thy foot against a stone

Thou shalt tread upon the lion and adder: the young lion and the dragon shalt thou trample under feet.

Because he hath set his love upon my, therefore will I believe him: I will set him on high, because he hath known my name.

He shall call upon me, and I will answer him: I will be with him in trouble; I will deliver him, and honor him

With long live will I satisfy him and shew him my salvation.

As a child growing up, I knew that I was truly loved by my parents. The all-endearing names they would call me: Cutie, Precious and Darling. This made life much more enjoyable even in hard times. Over the years, the family was transferred to different parts of the country. My favorite place was Discovery Bay, Jamaica. I loved the sea and the white sand beaches. In the early mornings, the fisher men could be seen coming with their catch of the day. Fresh seafood of all kinds. At nights, the waves could be heard, sometimes beating against the rocks. At other times, the calm soothing sound of the waves on the sea shore. One year during the summer holiday, I was able to visit for a short time. It was so much fun going to the beach and having fun with the other families. My father came back to get me, and we were supposed to leave the next morning. I asked him if we could stay for another day and he said, "yes." Our transportation going back home was a mule drawn cart. It was just after I asked my father if we could stay for another day, that a car just came along and killed the mule. I was so devastated; I was in shock. I also blamed myself for the death of the mule saying, "that if we had left as planned, that would not have happened." I was about nine years of age at the time this accident took place. My father consoled me telling me that, "The Lord would have it this way. And if we had left, there may have been greater consequences." I still felt sad. But seeing the way my father handled the situation, and how he tried to convince me that it was not my fault, I was relieved. Sometime after, my father got transferred to that district and the family took up permanent residence there.

Through all the adversities and disappointments, I have never heard my father questioned God. I was reminded of Job 27:6, "*My righteousness I hold fast, and will not let go: my heart shall not reproach me so long as I live.*"

In the latter part of my father's years, I remember him saying, "The Lord has blessed me more than my beginning."

Job 40:12 says, *"Lo the Lord blessed the latter end of Job more than the beginning."*

The first house that my parents lived in was in the center of the district on the main road surrounded by relatives. My father was the only Christian in that large family. He was told by one of his siblings, "It's the church that you are in that's the problem why you are not more successful." This remark did not faze my father in any way. My parents were neighbors to one of his brothers and his family. The houses were distances away from each other, but the smell of certain foods prepared in the kitchen that is not attached to the house seems to travel even further than food cooked in a kitchen attached to the house. There were times when things were hard, but you would never know it, when you smell my mother preparing food for the family. First, she would go to her garden in the back to get fresh tomatoes, Irish potatoes, and other things that were in season. And before long, she would have what I would call a delicious smelling meal ready. One day my Aunt-in-law smelled the food and commented, "You smell that big cooking that she doing over there?" Sometimes I wished people knew that we were poor. For instance; when they were giving free uniforms to the children in school, my brother and I did not get any. We were told that your parents can afford to buy uniforms. One day my mother happened to look outside and up towards the fence, there were some people surveying the land and my mother brought it to my father's attention. Upon inquiring the reason for this, my uncles said a part of my Father's land belonged to him; therefore he is taking what is his. My father sat in the house, calm, collective, said nothing and did nothing. Looking at the situation, some people thought that is a sign of **not** standing up and speaking out, but, 1 Timothy 6:6 tells us, *"but godlinesss with contentment is great gain."* I am sure this scripture is one of the most fitting in this situation. He lived a healthy calm Godly life. I can remember every year in the spring; he would get this bitter mixture together which is made from the bark of the bitter wood tree and other type of mixtures. He poured it into a bottle and took it for a number of days. With that cleansing of his body; along with regular fasting, praying and studying the word of God, he lived a very long healthy life. I do not say this in a malicious way, but these things are for our learning. My father outlived most of his siblings, and this should be in the forefront of our minds: 'We brought nothing into this world, and we cannot take it with us. Therefore, let us enjoy, share, live and let others live.

My father was offered a job by the richest and only Caucasian man in our area. This man had hundreds of acres of land and cows. He employed many people in different capacities. He offered my father a job to oversee the property, but he told my father that he would have to leave the church. We did not have to think about it, my father would not even consider leaving the church for the offer of a better job. It was puzzling as to why he made that request.

We lived in the same house until an opportunity came up for people in the district to obtain loans from the bank to build new houses or improve on existing houses. My parents could obtain one of these loans, and they built a nice little house on the same property. The house was admired by everyone in the district, by visitors and by the Governor who was passing through. He even inquired as to the owner of the house. Incidentally, my father's name and the Governor's name was almost the same except for one vowel in their names.

After we moved into our new house, my parents let the church use our old house to hold church services. Everything went well for some time, until all the people who got loans were told they had to pay the loans in full or they will lose their homes. One of our relatives who also obtained a loan to make an addition to his house said, "There is no way I am going to sit back and let them take my house." Somehow that relative, who had improved on his existing building instead of building a new one, could stay in his house.

As usual, my parents kept praying. But they eventually lost the house, and we ended up in a rented house which hit hard. But the scripture in 2 Corinthians 4:8 says, *"We are troubled on every side, yet not distressed; we are perplexed, but not in despair."*

After reaching the age of seven, my brother and I were fortunate to live across the street from the school we attended. The Principal of our school, who I spoke of earlier on, was a very young man who graduated from college at the age of nineteen years of age. Immediately after graduating, he became Principal of our school. Our school building was also used as a Baptist church for Sunday services.

Our Principal always speaks of his mother with such pride; how she instilled good values in him. She denied herself the necessities of life to send him to college. He spoke about the type of material she would recycle, from flour and rice sacks to make clothing for her, just to put him through college. He in turn expected the best from all the children in his school. He had the most beautiful penmanship, and good penmanship was expected in the school. It was not unusual for the paddle or belt to be used on students in those days. Also in those days, prayers were said in school in the morning before classes began, and at dismissal in the evenings. Grace was also said at lunchtime.

I remember the Principal asking my brother, why he failed the Second-Year Entrance Exam, because he knew that my brother can pass it. My brother told the Principal, that he was helping a girl with her Third-Year Exam, which she passed. The Principal reminded him that he was there to do his work and not the work of someone else. My brother was told to stretch across a bench, and the Principal took off his belt and taught him a lesson he never did forget. Those were the days when the saying 'It takes a village to raise a child' had real meaning. If we were seen doing something wrong by our neighbors, church members or friends of the family, it would be reported to our parents.

Our principal had practical training, daily exercise and competition on his priority list in addition to education. We would train for different types of sports, and once per year there would be a big completion where the best in that field of sport would be chosen to compete. I was very small in stature, but very agile. On the day of the finals, I was chosen to compete with a girl who I knew was a fast runner. She was much bigger in stature, but I had confidence that I could out run her. I was excited and ready to take home the prize.

The crowd had gathered in the big cricket ballpark across from our house. I was so glad my parents were there to see me compete in my first big race. My schoolmate and I ran the race, and I finished first and was given the trophy. That was my first time ever winning a race against this girl. I was so elated; this was my big day. My elation soon turned to deflation, when someone announced that my competitor had reached the finish line before I did. The school Principal, who was in charge, took the prize from me and gave it to my schoolmate, and gave me the second prize. I was very disappointed and thought about the way in which the adults made this hurtful decision. This was one of my very first real learning experiences as to how I am going to handle the situations that will arise in my life. Am I going to grow bitter or better? It did not affect the way I felt about my schoolmate. I even named one of my daughters after her. Approximately 56 years later, my schoolmate surprised me by attending my father's funeral. It was there I introduced her to my daughter who I had named after her.

Chapter 3

In all that my father went through, he still stood tall, and my mother was always right by his side. After many years of being a Pastor in his place of birth, he was transferred to another church with an open-air building. Being the type of giving person that he was, he gave the materials he had to build our house to the church to complete the building.

We were now living far away from the farm and my father had a long daily commute. It ended up being too much, and he sold some of the land and leased the rest to other farmers. From then on, it was strictly a faith walk for our family. In those days, most jobs were in farming and fishing. There was food, but money was scarce. I saw my father stand tall, never getting angry and never blaming anyone.

As the church started to prosper, my father was sent to start or revive churches in other districts without being given any financial help from the ministry headquarters. We were living in a rented house now and money was tight for my parents.

It so happened that our landlord was in the square, where the men would gather on Friday and Saturday evenings to play dominoes and talk about the happenings of the week. My father approached him to discuss the outstanding bill. And before my father got a chance to explain the situation; the landlord who was shorter than my father, reached up and slapped my father on the face. He then asked my father, "Where is the money for the rent that he owed?" This man was working on the impulse of the devil when he did this act; which ordinarily he would not have done, knowing that my father was a very well respected man in the community. That is why it is very important to have the flesh under control. How am I going to conduct myself in this situation? Am I going to retaliate; let the flesh rise, or am I going to let the Lord fight my battle. This could have caused damage to my father's reputation as a pastor; most importantly, causing a reproach on the church. Souls that were saved after that incident under his ministry may never have done so.

My father came home and told my mother what happened in the square. She asked him, "What did you do?"

My father responded, "What did you expect me to do?"

My mother said, "Defend yourself."

My father finally said, "You are forgetting that I have to get up and preach to the people tomorrow morning?"

This incident reminded me of the scripture in Matthew 5:39, *"But I say unto you, that ye resist not evil; but whosoever shall smite thee on thy right cheek, turn to him the other also."* One commentary says, "Bear it patently; give not the rude man as good as he brings and if proud fools think the worst of thee and laugh at thee for it, all wise men will value and honor thee for it." It was not easy to understand, but I learned a lot from that incident.

Before he was transferred, he started getting materials together to build us another house. But after seeing the condition of the place of worship where we were about to move to, and being the type of person that my father was, he used the material to make the new place of worship look better. Here again, my mother would say one of those, "But John" to my father; meaning, how could you use the material that was planned to start working on the house for something else? He always thinks that the work of the Lord and the house of the Lord come first. Growing up, I always thought that certain things that happened to us as pastors' children, was not common occurrence; just to find out that it was more common than we thought. Some years ago, I was surprised to hear a pastor's child; which I thought they were well adjusted, well accomplished and made great achievements, mention the drawbacks of his life as a pastors' child. I can attest to some of them; but now being much older, much wiser and much more experienced, I thank God for being the one to experience that type of life which is a great privilege.

It was always a fun time for the family when we went to the beach to swim. Because my parents were pastor and pastor's wife, it was not ethical for us to be on the beach in revealing bathing suits. But there were a few places on the beach where just one family could be accommodated. One day we went for a swim, and I jumped off the rock. On my way down into the water, I had a pain in the back of my leg. It was almost like a paralyzing feeling that would not stop. I found out later, that was a so called 'Charley horse.' I got scared; calling out for my father to help me. He dived down into the water so fast to rescue me, that I could not even remember entering the water. For the rest of that day, I stayed on the beach too scared to go swimming again. My parents had lived to be what we sometimes refer to as 'a good old age.' Although they have passed on to be with the Lord, I am still thanking God for them.

One of the parishes that my father was transferred to; I would consider the most difficult. My mother decided that she was going to Kingston to look for a job. She had an aunt there she could stay with, until the living conditions was worked out. Some time went by, and I decided I missed my mother, and that I was going to visit her. I did not have any money to go into Kingston, but all I could think of, was going to visit her. There were cars that would go back and forth into the city; they were called robots. The drivers would go as far as taking the passenger directly to their gate for an extra fee.

Sometimes the car would be so full of people. That day, I decided this is it. I stopped the car driver, told him that I wanted to go to Kingston and that I have never been there before. I also told him that I did not have any money to pay him, but not to worry because my mother will pay him. As we traveled over the country roads, he repeated in Jamaican dialect, "Make sure me get me money." There was absolutely no doubt in my mind, that he would get his money; I had that childlike faith. The driver had taken most of the passengers to their respective destinations. My very first time in the city, we saw the street I started looking for the number and there was my mother walking real fast coming through the gate. I called out to the driver, "There is my mother!" I could see the shock on her face and the love in her heart. I said, "Mama I missed you. I came to look for you." My mother paid the driver, and said she had to go right back to work; that she had just rushed home to take care of something, and was on her way back. If one more minute had passed, I would have missed my mother. Her aunt was at work; I did not know anyone else in the city, and I did not have the phone number of anyone. In my mind, I just thought, my mother will be there; she was always there. Even when the driver of the car kept reminding me about his money, I kept saying, "She will be there!" I am still thanking God for honoring my childlike faith. She took me straight to work with her. On visiting my mothers' place of employment, I met her employer. I also met a world renowned female singer who was visiting with them. She thought I was so pretty, and she asked my mother if she would allow me to go with her to visit her country. My mother did not give it second thought; her reply was no! I imagined my mother must have said, 'not my precious.' We may be going through our Lodebar (a dry season in the desert); 2 Samuel 9:4, but we are not forgotten. Shortly after, our family would get settled in Kingston. And like fate would have it, one of the same ministers that would come to our district to preach years ago, stayed in our house. We became like family. We met him in Kingston after all those years, and he in turn would be of assistance to our family. The kindness that my parents showed this minister and his wife years ago, came back to us.

There are times in our lives when we are observed by people more than we imagine. They can point out characteristics about us that we are not aware of, some good and some bad. When we are at the place where we can accept the good compliments with grace, and work on the bad ones with expectation of improvement, then we will realize that we are maturing in age in our spiritual walk with the Lord Jesus. I was just a teenager when I had my first summer job volunteering at a printing company in order to prepare for the working field. There was a young intelligent man who was an accountant at the firm. He was from Africa, spoke English fluently, and had one of the most beautiful penmanship I had ever seen. Someone in the office told me that he was a prince which I did not believe, she went on to say he was here until the war was over in his country. He did not say much to me in his conversations but apparently he was observing me. One day we were at work and a number of people dressed in beautiful African outfits came to visit him, they were bowing to him in salutation. That when I thought this is a fact, he is a prince. One day he finally approached me, informing me that he had been observing me, pointing out some of the characteristics he had observed in me and I could be an asset to his country. He invited me to go back to his country with him, which I appreciated both the compliments and invitation, but declined his invitation. The lesson I learned from this even at a young age, we are being observed, therefore strive in every way to set a good example.

Chapter 4

My father and family were transferred to the Parish of St. Andrew. Like all the other parishes, I wondered what awaited us. Would the people pick on us, because we were the preacher's children, as if we were living in a glass bowl? I was now a teenager and anxious to help my parents financially. A job opening came up at the postal agency for a Clerk to run the agency. I was under the age that was required to apply for this job. I was also a newcomer in the district and had no experience in this field. In addition, I had to be bonded by someone who had confidence in me. My father stepped up and signed the necessary papers. I was chosen to fill the position; for which I was eternally grateful. I had to walk to the nearest Post Office to get my training on how to operate the Postal Agency. Since I was new in the district, some of the folks did not understand why I was chosen for the post. I know for a fact that it was God's plan for me. I was very young, and I regarded my job with the utmost importance. Every month, my book balanced out with the number of stamps sold and other transactions that took place. Not everyone thought that would be possible. The compliments go to my parents.

I recall a young man who would walk all the way from his home in the adjacent District to the Post Office. He would stand outside the window of the Post Office and talk or socialize with the folks who came by to pick-up their mail. Finally, he thought it was time to pop the question. He asked me to lend him some money from the 'the government coffers.' I responded, "No way, I would not do it for myself, so why would I do it for you?" He left the district after telling the people, that I was not interested in men. I never saw him again after that. I set the record straight by letting them know that he was there on a different mission. He thought this young girl was nave. And when he realized I was not, he tried to paint a different picture of me. Temptations were hurled at me, but I left that job with my reputation intact. During my time spent in those beautiful hills of St. Andrew, I heard about the lush green picturesque scenery by the water filtration plant that was operated by male workers. I had never seen the plant. One day I was walking with my parents, when a lady accosted us. She told my parents, that her little girls; ages six and seven, were standing on top of the hill overlooking the path leading to the plant, and they saw me going to the filtration plant. I was caught with such surprise. I just kept repeating, "It wasn't me." Normally, there would be nothing wrong with going to the plant to enjoy the scenery and observe the filtration process. However, since we were pastor's children; now commonly known as PKs (Pastors kids), we were expected be aware of the message our actions would send, and to set a better example. Thessalonians 5:22 says, *"Abstain from all appearance of evil."*

I felt like I was in a court of law trying to defend myself. I reiterated that I was not there, and that I had never been to the plant. The woman insisted that her children do not lie; and to my shock, my father seemed to doubt what I said. Up to this point, my mother had said nothing. Then suddenly she said, "Daughter, I believe you." Those were some of the most precious and consoling words I had ever heard. This incident taught me, that sometimes fathers may not understand, but mothers often have such a bond with their children that they can tell when something is not right. My mother's words came at a time, where I was reminded of Proverbs 25:11, *"I word fitly spoken is like apples of gold in pictures of silver." A mother has the heart that cares completely, gives so generously, loves so deeply, has the faith that family's treasure, is supportive and kind, gives inspiration and advice, is concerned and sacrifices, senses our unspoken needs, makes a home a happy place and offers up to the Lord loving prayers and tears. A mother's heart aches when we are hurt. What would we do without caring and loving mothers?*

After this incident, my young mind started wondering why the girls thought they saw me at the water filtration plant. From the distance, where they lived to looking down at the plant, it's like looking across the Grand Cannon. I decided to do some detective work on my own. I asked one of the employees at the plant, if someone looking like me came there on the day in question. He immediately said 'yes,' and that she frequently passes by the plant on her way home. I investigated further by waiting to see her. Upon meeting her, I could see why the little girls thought that it was me. The resemblance was there; although, she was older than I was. I always try to learn something from my life experiences. And the one thing I learned from this incident was to be very careful about what we think and what we see, because we could be mistaken. My family had moved to another district in St.

Andrews, where we were quick to realize that 'The Hope Botanical Gardens,' was one of the favorite places for people to bask in the beauty of hundreds of different types of flowers, trees and perfectly manicured lawns. On this day, my younger sister went to 'Hope Gardens' as it's called. She was late getting home, so my mother told me to go and see about her; she should have been home already. Most of the visitors were on their way out of the gardens, because it was close to closing time. I was the only one going in the opposite direction, when I happened to see this handsome young man riding a bicycle on his way out. He was curious as to my reason for going the opposite direction since it was closing time. He assured me that almost everyone was out of the garden. After I got to know him I realized; that's his way of life. Not stand in line to be served, and always the last one to exit anywhere that is crowed. I thought this was just a co-incidence meeting this stranger, and did not think we would meet again. But he seemed to have had other plans locating me; which he was successful in doing. I was walking through the gate of our residence when I heard someone said, "There she is." When I looked around, he was riding in a car with a more mature looking gentleman who was driving the car. After finding out where I lived, he came to visit. He invited me on a date which I accepted. When he came to pick me up, I told him that my friend is coming with us. He stood there for a few seconds; apparently getting his thoughts together, then he gracefully bowed out and left. I thought this might have been a turn off for him; but apparently it wasn't, because he was back. I told him about a family member in the United States of America, who had suggested that I come for a visit to see how I would like it there. And if all went well, I would make it my home. He was very disappointed and mumbled, "Why do women always want more." Those remarks did not pertain to me; therefore, I ignored it. Well, he eventually won. I told him that he needed to speak with my father in regards to marriage. He did not hesitate. He had already met my mother, but my father who was working away from home at the time, came home. There! He finally met my father. And in the process of asking for my hand in marriage, he broke out into the biggest pile of perspiration on his forehead. I thought it was hilarious, but I felt bad for him. It was brought to my attention that someone tried to talk my father into not giving his consent to this marriage; telling him that these mix marriages never work. The only reason for that was that this young man was of a different ethnic background. My father was a very wise man. He let me know that all he wanted was for me to be happy. He went on to say, "If this is the man you have chosen, I will not stand in your way. He then gave me his blessing." I just loved my father for saying those words. My mother loved him from the first time they met. There had never been a cross word between my parents and my husband.

Chapter 5

It was now time to meet his father who was not told before-hand that I was of a difference race. I did not have the opportunity of meeting his mother, due to the fact that she had passed away. I honestly was not prepared for this. It brought a chill in our relationship. There was brief respite in our seeing each other. One night, I dreamed that someone handed me a beautiful bouquet of yellow gerberas. I got up the next morning and smiled, because I knew what that meant. In all of this, I did not have much to say. Because my philosophy was, 'Whatever will be, will be.' Reflecting on that chanced meeting at 'The Botanical Hope Gardens,' its name – botanical means: live plants, flowers and 'hope.' In some cases, that is all some people have. It is always refreshing to visit the garden; there is never a dull moment. New landscaping and new and exciting species of flowers and plants. I am sure a lot of folks find their 'Their soul mate' there as I did.

I was not prepared for my husband's snoring; it was like a freight train. Our neighbor; who was introduced to me as his mother's best friend, lived some yards away from our house. She jokingly said one day, "I can hear your husband snoring from over here." I knew that I could not sleep with that type of noise; therefore, I prayed a simple prayer. "LORD, please let my husband stop snoring." I left it in his hands. Some months went by, then out of the blue my husband stopped snoring. He would just let out a sound as if he is expelling air through his mouth. For the rest of his life; we slept together, and he had never snored. I know for a fact, that even when we are not serving the Lord as we should, he will still hear our cry.

When my husband and I were expecting our third child, I was feeling so sick and weak from the usual morning sickness. Things were not going right financially. My father stopped by our home. In a way, I thought it was wrong timing, but I was frustrated, sick and weak. I blurted out to my father, "I am leaving this man." My father never raised his voice at me. But at certain times when he spoke, I knew from the tone of his voice; especially when he would end with these words "that settles it," he meant what he said. I must have shocked him by my remarks. He said, "You chose that man, you stay with him." I did not think I would have thanked my father for saying those words, but I grew to appreciate him even more.

Looking back on the situation, I asked myself, "What was I thinking? I did choose that man for better or worst. After the wedding ceremony, the minister let us kneel. He prayed at such length, that I wondered about the long prayer. Over the years when there were such trying times, I reflect on that lengthy prayer; thinking, God was preparing us for the rough road ahead. Love, marriage and living together was an experience for me. I think a lasting relationship should include the 'agape love:

unselfish unconditional love for each other. Some time ago, a question was asked of the audience that I was asking myself, "How do you feel about having a best friend of the opposite sex in your marriage?" My answer was 'no;' which I was in the minority, leaving me wondering why. I came into the marriage with my husband having friends, which I thought he would still want to hang around with. I had a few friends, who I thought would still drop in occasionally. The word best; as we all know means, 'excelling all others.'

From the speaker's standpoint, those of us who said no was right. There should be friends; which we all need other than our families. Best friends are usually our confidant, one who we confide in with our innermost thoughts and secrets. This can cause a world of mis-understanding and breakup of marriages; some intentionally and in some cases unintentionally. In the early years of my marriage, I learn a valuable lesson. My husband consulted his siblings; included them in a plan that he had without mentioning it to me. I felt hurt, left out and disappointed. Needing someone to talk to, I turned to my family. Those who I know loved me, loved my husband; therefore, nothing but good could come out of this. That was fine, till my mother told her sister who was of a different temperament. Things got out of hand. And I was left asking myself, 'What in the world did I just do?' I had to find a towel to put out this fire that I started. With quick and thoughtful thinking, I tried to repair the damage. Looking back at the whole situation, I should have gone to my husband and let him know how I felt about been left out of his discussion making. I also felt that, if I confided in my mother, I should have asked her to keep this confidential. I learned a valuable lesson. After our last child started school, I talked it over with my husband in regards of going back to work out of the home; since with such a large family it would take some of the strain off him. My husband reluctantly agrees. We decided to employ a helper in the home; to pick up the slack. Things went well at work and home.

After six months, I was promoted to a supervisory position in our office; which was an asset in one way, a raise in salary but longer hours at work. One night my husband and I had a very big disagreement. So big, that I reached for a suitcase to take a few things and leave the house before the children heard the disturbance. I had purposed in my mind that when disagreement occurs; which they will, I did not want my children to hear those types of behavior. I finally got to the suitcase. And before I could get one item in, he begged like a baby, "Please don't go." We somehow called a truce, with the promise that I would not leave. The next morning it was time to get ready for work. I got my composure and left my problems behind with the intention of giving my best service with a smile. I got to work at 8:30am to find my Mother waiting at the door of the office. Now, she and my Father were ministering in a rural area miles away from where we lived. I was so shocked, I could not contain myself. I quickly asked her, what she was doing here and at this early time of the morning. She replied, "I had a disturbing dream about you, and I could not sleep the remainder of the night. I took the first bus out to get here." The awesome thing about this, is that my mother had been saying for years she don't understand why she cannot dream like she used to any more. I could not look my mother in the eyes when I replied, "I don't know why you had a dream like that, everything is fine." I lied, because of the incident that took place early on in my marriage. But when I looked into her eyes and heard her say in a soft motherly voice, "Cute." This dream was so real; thinking about the distance she had traveled just to come and see about me, I admitted to her that her dream was real; something did happen. But I was quick to let her know that my husband and I did have some disagreement, but it has been sorted out. Someone penned these words years ago, "Can a Mother's tender care cease towards the child she bears?" My answer is, 'if she has the heart of a real mother and her faculties are working right, her love will always be there.'

There was another time in my life that proved God's awesomeness and my protection. I was on my way to work, standing at the bus stop waiting for the bus. The time was ticking away and there was no bus in sight. Looking towards my right, I saw a friend of our family driving in my direction with a passenger in the front seat. I stepped forward to ask him for a ride to work. I took a second look, stepped back, because I saw where he was driving at excessive speed. The bus finally came. And I realized that I would be late for work, but I knew I made the right decision. When we got about two miles up the road, I looked to my left on the property which houses the University Hospital. There was the car, which the young man was driving sitting off in the distance, hanging from a tree; absolutely hanging from the tree. The entire day at work, I was a nervous wreck. The evening papers came out, and on the front page was this car hanging from the tree. The driver died, and the passenger walked away without a scratch.

The explanation about the car was that it was modified in a way that, at excessive speed it could lift off the road. The young man was a kind soft spoken family man with two young children, and their mother who was left to mourn such a tragic loss. He came home late the night before, and was awaken early that morning by a call from someone who needed a ride to work. The speculation is that the driver was not fully awake. I was in shock and in disbelief, wondering what would have happened to me, had I not changed my mind about asking for a ride to work. I also wondered why that young man would lose his life doing a good deed. I have concluded that some things are best left in the hands of the Lord; He has all the answers.

God has truly been good to me in every aspect of my life. He gave me a husband who loved children. My husband seems to have taken Psalm 127:3-5 to an exceptional level, *"Lo children are a heritage of the Lord: and fruit of the womb is his reward. As arrows are in the hand of the mighty man: so are children of the youth. Happy is the man that has his quiver full of them."* As with most things in life, we learn as we go. During my first three months of pregnancy, I got very sick. Most of the times, this was the clue that I was expecting a child. During those months, I lost so much weight, and felt so sick, that I don't have much energy and most of all I cannot eat. If I do, everything comes back up.

On one occasion when we were on our way to visit his father, we decided to take him some patties. He insisted no beef patties; therefore, we bought him sea food patties instead. I did not question it, and he did not explain why. After we got married, I realize that beef was not cooked or eaten in their home. Having missed all those years of not eating beef, I think he decided to catch up. He would bring home some of the finest cuts of grass fed beef for me to cook. I did not mind doing this. I was good at cooking, since my mother was a very good cook; both pastry and food in general. One of her favorite pastries was what she called 'the king's pudding;' which instead of baking, she would steam it. A smile always comes on her face when she said; 'Today we are going to make the king's pudding.' One day, my husband brought home this big piece of steak for me to cook. He went to work with the intention of coming to get his dinner. I got up to fix the dinner; every time I looked at the meat, I got sick and ran back in the bed. I kept doing this with the intention that I am going to feel better. This was in the late fifties; early sixties. We did not have a refrigerator, so everything we got straight from the market, we cooked the same day. As the day wore on, I just felt more sick and weak. The next time I looked at the beef, it started turning blue. We were in the process of digging a hole for the sewer system, so I threw the steak into the hole. That was the best thing I could think of at the time, since looking at the meat made me more sick.

When my husband came home, there was no empathy what-so-ever. There was one thing that he said that I did not think about, "Why didn't you ask the neighbor to fix it." He believed I did it on purpose because I did not want to eat it; therefore, I was not interested in cooking it. I was too sick to think straight. He slowly learned that things were real. I remembered one time; all I felt for was a salad tomato. I fixed dinner for the family, and he rushed to get me the tomato. He brought back one of the loveliest tomato I had ever seen. I inquired how much he had paid for it; because they were not in season, and he must have paid quite a bit extra. When I heard the price, I told him he should not have paid that much. His reply was, "I thought you wanted the tomato." We sat down to dinner. And while they were eating meat, I was enjoying the tomato. He said, "Is that all you are going to eat?" That was the best most refreshing tomato I had had ever eaten. I concluded that it was worth every penny. Over the years, I thought that there should be more information given to men as to the struggles we women endure. Especially those of us who have this terrible morning sickness; which in those days, we were told there was no help.

There was one good silver lining. At exactly three months after, it just disappeared. I could remember with one of my pregnancies, I got up feeling perfectly fine. After checking the calendar, I realized that it was exactly three months. We are now in a more advanced age with so much information available; it is truly a blessing. It was a struggle getting things in their right perspective. But life is an experience and experience is the best teacher. Six children with six different personalities; there was always something exciting going on.

Chapter 6

My husband loved his home and family. Some people would describe him as the homey type of person, who would go to work, come home to his family. He would also be described as 'A man that knows where to hang his hat.' I was told as a child, 'You look your best always, even if you do not have a lot of clothes.' Earlier in our marriage when he came home, my hair was combed, my clothes were clean. He stopped, looked at me, and then asked, "Where did you go?" I replied, "Nowhere." He then realized that he is not coming home to see someone looking like a drab. We are now living in the twenty first century, where women work out of the home more than before. Working out of the home gives us more time to get dressed up. But being in the home, is not an excuse not to look nice for our mate. This is my humble opinion! That is where some relationships go sour. The men are out in the work place most of the week, looking at ladies all dressed up. Then to come home and see the opposite, can leave question marks in their minds. It is not necessary to dress up as if going to a party; just in moderation

One of my husband's hobbies is to cook. That is one of the times that he and the children had the most fun; waiting to eat his very, very spicy meals. After they started to reach teenage years, their interests changed. The girls would be exploring different avenues; which included boys. That literally caused him to see red. This is where someone must keep a calm cool head. When the children were growing up, my husband and I were of different opinion when it came to disciplining the children. I was more like my parents; one stern look should send the message. He was very easy going with them. He would say things like, "Let the children express themselves." He changed his mind when the girls started to like boys. One day when of the girls rattled his nerves, he turned to me and asked, "What are you going to do about this situation?" I just smiled and said, "Let her express herself," which was not an appropriate answer, but it was something to put a damper on the situation at that time. Sometimes he could be so funny, but yet so serious. One day he brought a guitar home. I thought to myself, 'he is going to take up another hobby; learning to play the guitar.' Finally, he said, "This is for you." I had never played a guitar; never express the thought of learning to play one. Knowing my husband, I know there had to be some other explanation to this. I kept inquiring. And he just sat there in silence in the lazy boy chair that I had bought him, staring into space and shaking his legs which was one of his favorite things to do. When I realize that I was not going to get anywhere at that time, I dropped the subject until another time. One day when I thought the time was right, I sat down beside him and asked, "Why did you buy me that guitar?" He replied, "I bought that so you can learn to play it. Get a program on the radio, where you can sing and play the guitar. Let the people call in to the program, and then you won't have to be going back and forth to church day and night." Finally, there was my answer. I knew my husband well enough to know he had something up his sleeves. I admired the thought of him thinking about me, to buy me a guitar. It could be a way of propagating the gospel, if done with the right intentions. The word of God also tells us that, 'We should not forget the assembling of ourselves together. It's for a reason. We strengthen each other by our testimonies. We are gregarious creatures, and we need different types of people in our lives to make it complete.

There are times when my husband would not do the things that I asked of him, or do the things that he should have done. His favorite words were, "What's the hurry?" Over the years I had grown to realize, that is the way he is and nothing and no one is 'gonna change that. It's either that I nag him out of his mind, or use wisdom. I choose to use wisdom, but there are times when procrastination should be the last resort. Therefore, I would take things into my own hands and find a way to get things done.

I was brought up in a Christian home, but was not a Christian at the time. After my husband and I started having children, I found every excuse not to attend church. I was brought up in a home where whenever the church doors open the entire family is in church. Now that I had children, I sent them to church, but we did not attend. I would get up on Sunday mornings, make breakfast for the family, get all six children dressed and send them off to church. During this period of my life, I only went to church on special occasions. It got to the point when one of my children asked me, "Why do we have to go to church, and you don't?" My reply was, "Because my parents let me go to church and it's your time now." I did not tell them my parents took me to church, which is totally different. With the children out of the home, there was just enough time to clean up the house and prepare Sunday dinner.

Sitting down to a Sunday evening dinner with my family, was the most important meal of the week. After which, we may head for the botanical gardens or just sit and watch the children play in the front yard. And play they did. I can remember one incident where I bought a swing set, slide and everything that was included in the set. It was assembled, but not anchored in the ground. As I was walking inside the house, I turned around and to my shock all six children jumped on the swing set and the entire thing came down in a tangled heap of metal. There goes about five minutes of use of a brand-new swing set.

There is such a vast experience in raising a family. I think after doing so, we should be able to take on any other challenges that come our way. My whole life was centered on my family; from making

school uniforms and church outfits to meeting dead-
lines. At one point, I started thinking about where I
would spend eternity if I died. But quickly tell
myself, I will give my life to the Lord someday; but
not now.

My husband usually bets on the horses, but with
no more than two dollars. He was very careful
about his spending of money. He was so meticulous
about many things, and one was the way he put his
money together in his wallet. They would have to
be placed uniformly. I could remember him asking
me, 'Why I did not stack money that way.'
Although I am an organized person, I did not find it
necessary to place money in a specific order. His
opinion was that, 'It is people who do not regard the
value of money that places money in a helter-skelter
fashion.' He may have been right, because while he
was wagering not more than two dollars on the
horses. I started my wagering, but I was spending
more than he did. And I never won anything other

than a few dollars. Finally, one day I won some money. My horoscope had said, I would be having a good fortune that day. I decided to put my entire winning on a horse; except for two dollars that I gave to a friend. That friend came out better than I did, because my horse did not win.

Chapter 7

When the older children were teenagers, we decided to move from Jamaica to the United States of America. I migrated to Louisville, Kentucky. One of the things Louisville is most famous for is its horse racing. I was all excited about being right there by Churchill Downs, where I could bet on the horses and have fun. I hated being away from my family. It was one of the worst feelings that I have ever experienced. I was living with relatives, but I felt as if I was in a world all by myself. The Lord had pulled the rug from under me; separated me from my family, by taking away my security blanket, 'my family,' and left me bare. The void was so deep in my heart, that I could not stand it. God knows how to speak to our heart through even a total stranger.

One day I was on my way home from work, when I met a stranger carrying a bible. I commended him on taking the good book with him. I began to tell him that I was waiting for my family to join me in the United States, and how much I missed them. He advised me to start attending church before the devil started talking to me. I thought it was funny the way he said it, but it kept resounding in my ears.

I was attending different churches, but I told myself that the commitment part could wait. The Lord wore me out until I finally decided, 'this is it.' The time was now. I gave my heart to Jesus. I never got around to visiting Churchill Downs. I passed by there; sometimes twice a day, but never bet on the horses and did not miss it. As for the horoscope, that was history. I realized that everything we need is in Jesus.

There is no reason to go looking anywhere else. I could remember my brother-in-law writing to me, asking that I send him the names of horses that were potential winners. My answer to him was, "the only winner I can send you is JESUS." I also recall someone saying to me, 'You are in a different category. Some folks leave Jamaica, lose their salvation and forget about God, but you came here and found Him." It seemed that way, but the Lord was waiting patiently until I got to the point where I fully realized that, I must go His way to have a fulfilled life.

Personnel at the American Embassy told me, that I had to get a job and save a certain amount of money for my family to join me. This was one challenge that I gladly accepted. I met the challenge and went back to get my family; just to be told by the Embassy that only my husband can leave, and he would have to get a job to show proof of additional income. I was truly devastated with both of us leaving the children. The blessing in all of this was, that my parents who were living close by gladly agreed to move into our home and care for the children.

Within three months, I went back to Jamaica to get my children. I arrived in the evening, with the intention of flying out the next day with the children. When we got to the airport, I was told that our seats were not reserved, because I had forgotten to call and confirm my flight. I sat in the airport thinking this could not be happening. Transportation to and from the airport was challenging; especially with so many children. All I could do is stay calm and pray. The plane took off without us. We sat there in silence. I thought the airline staff had forgotten us, because there was no further communication regarding our departure.

The staff may have forgotten us, but God had not forgotten us. While we were sitting in the airport, an airline pilot came over to us and told us that there was an empty air plane going to Louisville, Kentucky; our intended destination. He told us that we are welcome to ride with him, if we so desired. I honestly thought I was dreaming. Again, God's mercy was right on time. He always steps in when things are brought to the last extremity. Surrounded by my children, I realized that I had to think in multiples, and not just for myself. I had asked the Lord for help with the hope that somehow He would make a way, and that he did in a mighty way.

Seeing that pilot coming over and uttering those words to me, reminded me of the Gospel of Acts Chapter 12:13, 'When Peter was in prison and prayers were going up by the saints for him. God sent His angel in the prison to Peter. The angel escorted Peter out of the prison.

When Peter came to his conscious self he said, "Now I know of a surety that the Lord hath sent His angel, and hath delivered me." The people who were praying for Peter were also shocked.' We gladly entered the aircraft and sat in the middle section. The flight crew told us we were welcome to come up to the first-class section. When God does something, he does it in first class style. It was as if he had chartered the plane just for my family. Those were some of the many angels I met throughout my life.

Another angel that was sent to help my family in one of our trying moments was, Mr. John Rayburn of Child Protective Services. I am forever reassured that there are angels in human form that the Lord sends our way to get us out of tight spots. And also to remind us that He will never leave us nor forsake us.

Matthew 28:20, *"Lo I am with you always, even unto the end of the world."*

Sometimes we are battered by the storm, and we are so busy rolling around in self-pity and not focusing on God's promises. He is right there waiting to get our attention.

When we started walking, we could see His foot prints walking with us; only to take another look and see only one set of foot prints. This is the time when doubt sets in. We finally question the Lord, 'Why?' Only to be reassured that He was there all the time, and the one set of foot prints was His. He was cradling us in His arms and carrying us.

My family had settled and gotten acclimated to living in a new country. One evening my husband and I came home from work, and upon entering our house, we immediately noticed that the couch that was sitting on the north side of the room was moved to the west side. I asked why the couch was moved, but the answer did not make much sense; especially since the new position made it uncomfortable to watch the television. I told the children to put the couch back in its original position, but weeks went by and they never did.

It was unusual for the children to disobey me. Their father was more relaxed and would overlook things more easily, but I was stricter and they usually responded immediately. Sometime had passed, and the couch was still setting in that area. I finally decided not to mention any more about the couch.

On December 31, 1980 in Watch Night Service, I was interceding to the Lord on behalf of my family. Tears came streaming down my face, and a sister in the service asked me if everything was all right. I reply, "Sure, it's just that my family is weighting so heavily on my heart, and I had to cry out to the Lord for them." I went home, and when I walked through the door, I noticed that my husband looked worried. He said that the police are on their way to the house. Then he showed me the couch with six bullet holes in it. The bullets had penetrated the wall on the west side of the house. Right then, I realized why the children moved the couch to the west side of the room, and why they never put it back in its original position.

The Lord knew what was going to happen and protected us by having the couch block the bullets; saving my family from being hit. After the police investigation, we were told that the neighbors fired their gun while celebrating the New Year. It seemed silly to me; because if that was the case, they would aim up in the air instead of towards the house. There was, and still is no doubt in my mind that God has his angels surrounding us that no demons can penetrate us.

We thought it was a miracle for six gunshots to penetrate the wall. And even more strange, that all six shots lodged in the couch and no one was harmed. I was reminded of Psalms 34, "*The angel of the Lord encamped round about them that fear Him and delivereth them.*" We kept that couch for many years. And when I decided to get rid of it, one of my family members said she wanted it in their house, because it represents a miracle from God.

God promises are true. Psalm 3:5 says, "*I laid me down and slept: I awaked for the Lord sustained me.*

I will not be afraid of ten thousands of people that have set themselves against me round about."

Looking back over my life, I can truly see where the Lord was molding and preparing me for other mountains that I would have to climb, and obstacles I would have to navigate through.

It is amazing how things that we long for, wish they would be and pray for; suddenly one day the Lord just opens the way, and here they are. I was brought up singing the old songs written by 'Fanny Crosby,' who is a true inspiration to us all.

The scripture in Psalm 32:8, "*I will instruct thee and teach thee in the way which thou shalt go: I will guide thee with mine eye,*" must have meant a lot to her.

She was met with adversity at a young age, but became a song writer and poet; writing thousands of songs and hymns that encouraged, strengthened, inspired and brought joyful sounds all around the world. Some of the most beautiful songs with meaning were composed by her. 1Corinthians 14:15 reminds us, to sing with understanding. I also think of other writers who wrote beautiful songs that have been a blessing; strengthening and encouraging us.

Over the years, I have noticed that the songs being sung in the churches were more on the contemporary side. I started longing for the old songs and hymns. Thinking I was the only one with that yearning to hear these songs; one day I was reading the Louisville Courier-Journal newspaper, there I read where a lady wrote an article saying how she missed the singing of old time hymns in the church. It went straight to the core of my being; just to know that I was not the only one who had that yearning.

I placed the article in my Bible and whenever I opened the Bible there it was. I carried it around for years. Some time went by, and we got a new Pastor at our church. I was pleasantly surprised to hear the old songs being sung in the church again. The Pastor and his wife were not older folks, but being from the family of Bishops and long standing members of the church, they were exposed to all aspects of worship and songs. I remember so clearly one Sunday, the Pastor started to sing a song that I had not heard since I was a child. It was one of my mother's favorite songs. I busted out singing in that high soprano voice; it sounded so much like my mother. I thought it was my mother singing through my vocal chords. Tears of joy came streaming down my face. I was totally convinced that it was an answer to my prayer. God knows the very intent of our hearts, and he cares about every minute detail.

As a child; on Sunday afternoon after church, my favorite thing after dinner was to take the song books that we use in church services and sing the songs. I knew most of the songs that were in the books; some of them I could sing from memory. There weren't much musical instruments around. The most common one was a guitar, and the guitar player could read the musical notes. After putting a choir together, it was a joy listening to the sounds of the Soprano, alto, tenor, bass distinctive voices blending together. Although I cannot read music notes; over the years, I can still recognize a wrong note or off timing.

After the unpleasant incident on New Year's night, my husband decided that we had to get out of that neighborhood. We consulted a real estate agent, who showed us two houses across from each other. We decided on the most spacious one. With such a large family; it was not large enough, but getting out of the area we were in was our top priority. To our disappointment, someone out bided us on the house that we chose.

We ended up taking the smaller house. The lack of space was frustrating, but we lived and hoped for better days. Around the first Christmas after we moved into that house, someone thought they were more unfortunate than us. Therefore; while we were away from home, they broke into the house and took the television and all the Christmas presents. I thought it was ridiculous, but funny.

It reminded us of when we received our independence in 1962 from the British government. The economy in Jamaica went down and the price of merchandise skyrocketed so high that we decided 'no Christmas presents.' It was as if history was repeating itself, but in a different way, "'No Christmas presents,' someone else helped themselves to the things that were bought for the family.

One day; our first child who has a very inquiring mind, came home very excited. Telling us that the house two doors down from us is for sale, and that she had decided for a real estate agent to come that night and speak with us about it. I immediately asked my daughter if she was trying to embarrass us, knowing that we did not have the type of down payment for that size house. Her answer was, "It will not hurt to let the real estate agent come and talk with us."

He came as she planned. He looked at the papers for the house we were living in, and told us to our amazement, that we had enough equity built up to make a down payment on the house that is for sale. The owners were a very young couple who had just graduated from college. The husband, a veterinarian, bought the house with the intentions of getting a permit to operate an animal clinic on the premises.

It was a very spacious home, with a big fenced yard in the back. The neighbors objected to the Doctor having an animal clinic there, so the permit was not granted to him. It was all in God's plan, because we ended up getting the house. We stayed in that house until our children grew up and left home.

Chapter 8

In leaving our country of origin, it is amazing the different transitions that we must go through. In some cases, different languages, eating habits; some of us from a tropical climate to four distinct seasons and very cold winter months. One of my main problems was, having to wear the heavy outfits during the winter months. Being small in stature, I felt weighed down with coats and winter boots. I tried to avoid all those clothes, which had caused me on several occasions to put my health in jeopardy.

There was one time when I was racking the leaves during the fall month, I got hot and uncomfortable; therefore, I took off my bulky sweater. And with only a tee shirt on; I felt so good, not realizing that I was setting myself up for pneumonia. I got so sick, that I had to see the doctor; especially, since I was in the process of traveling to Jamaica to get my family to the United States. I was shocked at how fast I recovered from this illness after entering the different temperature out of the cold weather into a warmer part of the country.

I remember going on a trip from Louisville and traveling to Chicago. The weather was nice and warm in Louisville. Upon entering Chicago, I was hit by the most bone chilling windy weather; again I was not dressed appropriately. When we moved into this beautiful house, there was a big rose tree in the front of the yard. The first year, this rose tree produced a lot of flowers. We had a cold winter and the tree had died; so we thought.

Then came spring, and I suggested to my husband that we dig up the tree and put a new one in its place. We uncovered the roots, and to our amazement the plant underneath the ground was alive; just waiting to spring forth. We placed the dirt back over the roots, and sometime after came green leaves. In the month of June, the plant started to send forth its buds. Then it was covered with flowers. We spent twenty-five years in that home that God had given us, and that we loved so much. From that rose plant and other flowers that I planted, I made many floral arrangements. I would take them to the church that I attend or give them for someone who just needed a little act of kindness.

One Sunday, I took an arrangement to church. I had not completely made up my mind as to who I should give this floral arrangement to. For some reason, there was a young lady in the church who had a husband and five children. She would speak, if spoken to and was the type of person, who could be easily overlooked because of her reserved demeanor. During the time of putting the arrangement together, I kept visualizing giving the flowers to her, but I still had doubts in my mind.

I took the flowers to church and up came the young lady; I gave it to her. She had the biggest smile on her face. And then she said, "This is my last Sunday attending this church." It was then I realized, it was the Lord directing me specifically to that young lady. It could have been one of the other hundreds of people in the congregation, but she was singled out. And I was glad that I followed that leading. I must admit it's not all the time that I am obedient to that acting on these overwhelming urges. I had an article of clothing which I thought someone younger should be wearing. Immediately this young lady came to mind. I placed the article of clothing in my vehicle and drove around with it for weeks with the intention of giving it to her.

One Sunday morning, the young lady came to me and asked, 'If I had one of the same articles of clothing that I could lend it to her.' I was in awe. That article of clothing was in the vehicle; out of sight for weeks. In addition, I don't know of anyone driving around with things like that for just a spur of the moment thing. I gave her the article of clothing and told her that I intended was to give it to her for some time now.

Previously, I spoke about the transitions we go through when migrating to another country. The cold weather that some of us do not care for; there is still some pleasant things to look forward to. For instance, taking a ride through the countryside on an autumn day; priceless! Different types of trees; different colors ranging from yellow to deep rich golden brown can be seen for miles and miles.

The picturesque views have never cease to amaze me of the awesomeness of God's wonderful works. *Psalm 19:1, "The heavens declare the glory of God*; and *the firmament showed his handy work."* God is the one who sets the constant revolution of the year and its seasons in place.

The earth to bring forth her buds, and the garden caused the things that are sown in it to spring forth.

In every aspect of my life, I can see the Lord's handy work. From when I was a child, I would dream a lot. Some mornings, I would wake up feeling exhausted from traveling or flying in my dreams. The awesome thing is that, a lot of the dreams came through just as I saw them in the dreams. Dreams are sometimes described as a train of thought; or as imaginary transactions which occupy the mind during sleep. Living in an earthly body; we have as the background of our being, a dim region out of which our thinking labors forth to the day light which must come forward. While we are sleeping, we can only come to fully know what the dreams mean by looking back afterward we have awakened from the dream. Dreams and visions are frequently mentioned in the bible, and were sometimes used as a warning, encouragement or revelation.

On many occasions, I have had dreams that as soon as I awoke and told my family, it would become realty. One morning, I was telling my husband and my mother about the dream I had last night. I saw where my aunt's husband had died. I thought it was unfounded since he was not sick. While I stood there telling them about the dream, my aunt came to inform us that her husband had died. It was so unbelievable. During those days,' telephones were not readily available as they are now. Therefore, each one would pass the word on.

Some of the most pleasant and enjoyable dreams, are the ones in which I am flying or swimming. If I am being chased by someone; cornered in some unpleasant situation and got away by out-flying or out-swimming the adversary, it was a dream that left me feeling triumphant. I have recently learned that these dreams of me flying, is more directed to my own situation. Whatever the reason, it sure feels good to out fly my opponent. After a while, some family members got turned off; not wanting to hear my dreams.

It did not upset me in any way. Joseph's family in Genesis chapter 37 was upset about his dreams; not for the same reason, but I imagine my family members that did not want to hear, feared the dreams; having been so forthright. There was another dream, where I saw a death in the family. The individual was not revealed to me; but in the dream, it rained so hard and rained for days. I awoke and told my family the dream.

Sometime after, news came to my father that his brother had died. My parents went to the funeral. It rained so hard and long, until my parents had to come back without witnessing the burial. My uncle lived in a district where the soil is clay. This type of soil was sometime used to make pottery, because it is so hard for water to seep through. The more they tried to remove the water from the grave, the more it got filled up again. They just had to let nature take its' course, and wait until the water subsided. When I had the dream, I had no clue as to where this place was. I had visited my uncle's home only once, and to see the dream just fall into place the way it did was amazing.

There was another dream, where our oldest son was driving our car to work and he met an accident. I saw it in the dream so vividly. I got up the morning, and asked my husband not to let our son drive the car. My husband went ahead and gave our son the key. Within about fifteen minutes, our son was back to inform us that he was in an accident. When we saw the car, it was unbelievable that he walked away without a scratch. The car was totaled. Thank God for prayers, and the angels that are assigned to protect us.

This occurrence was not a dream, and this was the first time that it had happened to me. I always sleep on the right side of the bed closest to the wall, and my husband sleeps on the left side. There was a space between my side and the wall. My eyes were closed, but I was not asleep. I felt someone touched my right shoulder. I knew it was not my husband, because he was on the left side and was asleep. I quickly turned around to see a short Caucasian looking lady standing beside me. I was scared out of my wits. But she said, "I am not here to hurt you, but your daughters are in danger. They need to get away from where they are." I could not sleep and could not awake my husband, because he would think I am losing my mind.

Here again when no one else understands, there is a friend that does, and his name is Jesus. We can talk to him anytime; whether day or night. In this case, two of my daughters who had moved out of town, returned to visit with friends that they had known before they moved away. I would have preferred if they had stayed at our house, but they are grown and wanted to enjoy their friends. Most importantly, we trust their thinking that they knew what was expected of them. I did not want to call them; my intention was to visit in person. My problem was that I had to go to work, and then I would go there in the evening. I was on pins and needles all day. I went straight to where they were staying, told them to get out of there immediately; which they did. I knew that this experience was from an angel; nothing to be taken lightly. It took some time before I was told by one of my daughters' what the situation was about.

Psalms 34: 7, "*The angel of the Lord encamped around about them that fear him, and delivereth them.*"

Proverbs 3:5-6, "*Trust in the Lord with all thine heart; and lean not unto thine own understanding. In all thy ways acknowledge him, and he shall direct thy paths.*

Some years ago, I started having discomfort in my body. My Doctor detected the problem, and I was scheduled for surgery. Before I went into the hospital, I requested prayer from the folks at the church that I attended.

Shortly after, someone approached me with information on how to save money on not paying a big hospital bill; by diverting my money into someone else's name. I realize that I was going against my Christian principles; therefore, I flatly said "I will never do this." We talk about living by faith, depending on the Lord, the cattle on a thousand hills belong to us, and I could go on, and on. But when my faith is put to the test, I cannot afford to fail him.

I went in to have my surgery and everything went well, which I was thankful to the Lord for. I was told that before I am discharged, someone is coming to do a routine check on me. Looking at the television in my room, I could see from the weather forecast that it was freezing cold outside. I went over to the large window in my room; looking down from the fourth floor, my eyes were focused on a man dressed only in a lab coat. I thought to myself, 'Isn't it too cold to be wearing a light coat?'

Shortly after that, the same man entered my room. He introduced himself, and told me that he was here to be sure that the surgery did not leave any ill effects. I noticed that he had a bad cold; he went as far as apologizing and proceeded to the bathroom to wipe his nose and wash his hands. He examined me, which included close contact in my face. Sometime later, instead of getting discharged, I started getting sick. I had a high fever and just started getting worst. The doctor and nurses gathered around me trying to get my temperature down, which was extremely high. I happen to glance through the glass door, and there was my pastor and two of his assistants from our church who came to visit me standing at the door. They were told that no one can come in.

I later learned that our pastor went back to the church and announce for prayer, because I was very sick. I did not know how sick I was, until no one was allowed in my room. The surgery which should have taken three days in the hospital has taken a completely different route.

One night I had a dream seeing myself in a dark hole. I happened to look up, and saw this huge arm reaching down towards me to lift me out of the pit. His legs and arms were of a bronze color; his shoes were of the same color, as if he was wearing an armor. The thing that caught my eye most to all was his size; just huge and so strong looking. He lifted me out of the hole, after which I started feeling better. On the tenth day, I asked to be discharged. I left on the eleventh day, with a big bill brought on by someone else's mistake and no medical insurance. I asked for a reduction on my medical bill, but was told that my husband had a business and could afford it. Looking back over the whole situation, I do think this was a test from the Lord to see if I would sell out.

Money is an important thing in my life; but not the most important thing. I was overjoyed to have my health back, and my relationship with the Lord intact. I could pay my bill in monthly installments. Sometime after, my husband passed away. There was a balance of one thousand dollars left on my bill. I received a letter from the hospital telling me that they are aware that my husband had passed away, and they have written off the balance of one thousand dollars. I was grateful for any help; large or small if it is done honestly. Most of all I thank God for life. I am still poor in life's worldly goods, but rich in spiritual blessings. 1 Tim. 6:6 tells us, "But godliness with contentment is great gain." Now for my life; I am at the threshold of celebrating my seventy-ninth birthday, and I will say as a dear saint in our congregation use to say, "It's just Jesus."

As a child growing up, I have seen so much on the spiritual side, and on the worldly side which leave me thinking, is the Lord saying, "Did you learn from that situation?"   My husband and I were so different in so many ways, that I know that it was the Lord, the blessings of my parents, the long prayer that the minister prayed when we got married and our love for each other that kept us together.

Chapter 9

We both were good at cooking, and decided to open a restaurant. The plan was for me to quit my job, work in the restaurant full time. He would work part time in the restaurant, and part time at his job, still have income coming in from his business since he was an entrepreneur. The plan was geared to be successful with the restaurant, and then we would concentrate on him coming full time into the restaurant business. The transition would not be hard, since we owned some taxi cabs, and he drove one. If things worked as planned, he would hire another driver for the cab he was driving.

When I handed in my resignation at my place of employment; one of my co-worker said to me it will never work for wives and husbands to work together. I looked forward to working alongside my husband and I was not fazed in any way at her idea.

We have had difference of opinion, but never any knockdown, drag out fights.

We got compliments about our food, and started getting catering requests from surrounding churches, also wedding cakes requests. Over a period, we were hit by rate hikes, and other expenditures. My husband decided to spend more time on his job to re-coup what we were losing on my side of the business.

I knew my husband well enough to realize that it would not be long before he would be asking, 'About my intention regarding the restaurant, and losing money. I could hear his voice even before I got home asking, "How did we do at the restaurant today?" What disturbed me is, that in the past if there was a problem, financially, or otherwise, I could always fill in the gap by trying to solve the problem on my own. Now, I had to completely depend on my husband for all financial help. It caused me to take a closer look at myself. The Lord had brought me to a place where I realize that I could not fix everything on my own; marriage is a partnership.

I finally decided to sell the restaurant. I was fortunate to get someone to buy the business instead of just closing the doors. It helped us to re-coup some of our losses. The potential buyer told me that he did not have all the finances. His father was going to provide some help but he didn't have all the money on hand.

In reality, he wanted the entire building and he told the owner so. Time went by after he took over the business. I was driving in the area with my grandchildren on my way from church, and I decided to stop by and see how the new owner was doing. I entered the door, and my first impression was, 'What a difference!' The owner spent quite a bit of money to renovate the place. His decor was above what I could do financially. I am always glad for the accomplishments of others. Our minister taught us to pray for others, and the blessings would return to us. Such was David who prayed for his enemies, and the blessings returned unto him. I said in the hearing of my grandchildren, I wish I could have fixed up this place as nice as the new owner did. My oldest granddaughter; who was about ten years old at the time immediately said, the place may look nice but I bet he can't cook as good as you. She caught me off guard by making that statement. It left me with several thoughts in my mind. Never underestimate a child's thinking. It could be that she was wrong; perhaps he could cook better than I did, but that was positive thinking on her part. Also the right word at the right time makes such a difference. The age of the one who utters is irrelevant. This granddaughter was not a child that talked much, but there was another time when she gave me a surprise. All the grandchildren were riding with me home from church. I had to take a different route in a strange neighborhood. It seemed as if I was going around in circles. Finally

I said, let me try this way. My granddaughter spoke up and said, "You are going the right way." I asked her how she knew. She replied, "You have taken us this way before." I thought to myself, 'How could she had remembered; it must have been a long time ago. She kept directing me, until I reached the main highway. There are so many lessons to learn in life, and a lot comes from children.

The new owner of the restaurant had borrowed a ladder from me when he was renovating the place. I thought it was time for him to return it. I kept calling him, but there was no answer. I thought it was strange; could he be that busy at the restaurant? I then called a neighbor of his to pass on the message about retrieving the ladder. The neighbor told me that the business has been closed, because the owner was in trouble with the law. It turned out that I had gained more out of the business than the present owner. David said in Psalm 73, 'When he looked at the prosperity of the wicked, his foot almost slipped.' We sometimes feel that way; not knowing that things are not always as rosy as they appear to be, but God will show us in 'His time.'

Reflecting over my life, I can truly say that I am blessed. There are times when we will question, 'Why me Lord?' Those are the times when the storms of life seem to be beating on us so violently, that we are waiting for the breaking of the dawn; not realizing that we have not passed through those storm clouds yet. Those were just the waves that were beating on our storm-tossed ship. Finally, we are heading into the valley and the clouds are hanging so low. It appears as if there is no way out, but there comes a light at the end of the tunnel. It is the breaking of the dawn. There is that tired body and that exuberant spirit looking back and wondering, 'How did I make it over?' When we quote the words "I am blessed," let us remember that it is not just material things that we are talking about. It is the courage, and strength to believe God and to take Him at His words. When things do not go the way that we think it should go, we should accept the leading of the Lord; knowing that He is in control. Winning the battle is being submissive to His will. We are living in the twenty first century; these are not popular words, but I have seen Him work in different areas of my life. I am not referring to being used as a door mat for everyone to wipe their feet on. There are times when you know without a doubt, that things should be done the opposite way. But for peace sake, peace of mind, to save money on doctors' visits and for pent up feelings which can create ulcers in our body, let us replace it with love and submissiveness. Let us face the facts. If we believe that the bible is the infallible Word of God, then we realize that everyone must submit at some time in their lives. The highest order of the land must submit to the King of Kings.

For many years, my husband would bring home his paycheck and tell me to spend whatever is necessary, and to save the remainder of it. Everything was always taken care of; especially, since I did not like for us to have outstanding bills that were due and not paid in a timely manner. When I became a Christian, my husband decided that I would get enough money to pay the bills and for other necessities. I realized that he was being fed the wrong information about church and the money. One of my motto is 'God saves fools, but he does not keep fools.' Therefore, I had to act wisely. One day unexpectedly, my husband handed me a large sum of money asking me to keep it for him. It was as if a voice spoke to me, and I decided not to put the money in the bank; just had it ready when needed. I decided to place the money under the mattress. Every night we went to bed, we were sleeping on the money. One day my husband came home from work and said, "I would like to get the money." I went straight towards the bed, lifted the mattress, removed the money and handed it to him just the exact way he had given it to me. I could see the shock on his face, as he immediately counted it. It was all there. I went for a walk to clear the air. Upon returning, my husband handed me almost half of the money and said, "This is yours." I thought about what would have happened, if I did not use wisdom. When Solomon was anointed to become king, God inquired of him in dream as to his wishes. Solomon asked for an understanding heart. God in his infinite mercies knew that he would also need wisdom to reign over the people. In our daily relationships with people, we need insights to see into the situations and foresight an act of considering the future. The way we act will tell a lot about whether we are positioning ourselves to sink or swim.

I was married for quite a number of years, before I realized that a lot of men; including my husband, do not stop to ask for directions. My husband and I were about to take a trip out of town, when one of my daughters who had just bought a new car suggested that we drive her very low mileage car. She worked close to home and did not do much driving; therefore, she thought that would be good for the car to be driven some distance and on the highway. Her only request is that we do not let the car get low on gas. We started off fine. I felt confident with my husband by my side. All I had to do is sit back and enjoy the scenery of the countryside. My husband had the directions to our destination, and he is an excellent driver; and was very knowledgeable on the makes and models of cars. We kept traveling and traveling. I could not contain my thoughts any longer so I finally asked him, "Where are we and how far are we from our destination?" His answer was, "I am not sure." I suggested that we stop and ask for directions. He kept driving and driving. Finally, I told him that the next place that we come to where there is any form of habitation, I was going to get out and ask for directions. Finally, we saw a little town with one shop. I told my husband to stop for me to get directions. I went in and explained to the shopkeeper where we were attempting to go. He informed me that we were fifty miles out of the direction that we are supposed to be heading in; therefore, we had to go back fifty miles, then head in the right direction. We finally reached our destination, but it was late in the evening. Therefore, we had just enough time to turn around and head back home. I reminded my husband that we needed to stop and fill up on gas. That was when it got strange. He kept saying, "Yes, we are going to stop," which he did not. Finally, the car stopped. It was dark and there was no sign of any type of buildings around. We were fortunate to have the car out of the road, because the vehicles were whisking by leaving that trail of breeze as if they were going to blow us off the side of the road. It was such a desolate area that it could be considered as 'no man's land.' We had no way of contacting anyone, but as always God had his angels around us. A vehicle that was going in the opposite direction, stopped on the wide median which divided the road. I could not comprehend how he saw us over there on the other side of the road in the dark. He ran across the road in our direction; dodging the fast-moving vehicles. I was overjoyed to see someone coming to our aid. He asked if he could assist us. What struck me is that he did not look to see who we were. It was dark, and all he saw was someone in desperate need of help. The gentleman took us in his car, informing us that the nearest gas station is in the direction where he is coming from. They could get some gas, take it to the car and get it started. My husband must have been having a man to man talk with this kind stranger. Because when they came back with the car; while I was waiting for them at the gas station, the gentleman walked up to me and said, "Your husband said, the first thing my wife is going to say is, I told you that the car is out of gas." I just quietly said, "I did not have to tell him, he knew that the car was out of gas." Getting upset sometimes is a waste of time and energy. I thanked that precious stranger that God sent our way to help us. When we finally got home, it was almost time for me to go to work. So I just sat in a chair, until it was time to take a bath and leave for work. My husband was much fortunate, because he did not have to punch a clock. Therefore, he could get some sleep.

After hearing other couples talk about their husbands, I realize that some men would rather go around in circles or pretend as if they know where they going, than to stop and ask for directions. Thank God for technology. There are so many things that are designed to make life much easier than before. There are equipment's that are available on the market that comes with the correct information that will get us to our destination. There is nothing like a Global Positioning System (GPS). They are 'God sent;' especially for individuals who would prefer to go out of their way in the wrong direction, and then must turn around and go back on the right path. It saves time and energy, and makes for a better and happier relationship.

It has always been said that women talk a lot more than men. We crave more attention than men. And when we get these urges, we think there should be instant reciprocation to our desires. If this is not done, it's sometimes misinterpreted as not being loved. I watched a program on television recently, where the doctors invited their audience to ask questions. One young man asked, "Why do women talk so much; especially, when he wants to sit and watch a ball game. The doctor explained the physiological difference between a male and a female, and why we tend to think and act different. Realizing the differences in behavior, I had often tried to give my partner 'his time, break and space.' To have a happy relationship, we must accommodate each other. Sometimes we may think that because our partners do not express themselves verbally, that they do not love us. It may be a matter of the way they were brought up as a child. But if they truly love you, it will reflect in their actions. Many years ago, I had a car that started to have mechanical problems. The farthest thing from my mind was getting another car. One day my husband said, "Let's go get you a good car, because that car might break down soon." I realize that he was concerned, but said nothing about it. He gave me the opportunity to choose the car that I liked. It was a pastel blue Maxima; one of the first editions. We were asked if we wanted to get insurance on the balance that would be owed on the car, and we said no. I went to pick up the car the next day, and the salesman said your husband was here. I asked him, 'Why my husband came back?' And he said your husband's words were, "My wife would never forgive me if something happen to me, and she was left with this outstanding bill." I thought that it was strange that my husband did not mention to me that he had changed his mind. Even more strange was that he made the remarks regarding the possibility of something happening to him. I went as far as saying; this is just extra spending. I asked my husband about his trip to the car dealer, the insurance, and why he made those remarks, but there was no logical reason. I went on to say, "You know that we have been through thick and thin and we weathered the storm, so why would you make that remark?" With no response, it was as if I was talking to myself, so I just drop the subject. I still wondered it in my mind, why my husband acted the way that he did. Within eighteen months of getting me the car, my husband passed away. The shock of his passing was enough to send me in a tailspin. It was a very sad time to say the least. It took a while but after the dust settled and experiences were flashing before my very eyes. I realized that it was not a coincidence; it was all in Gods' plan. Our Heavenly father; in His wisdom, sees and knows far beyond what we would ask or think. I thank Him for His mercy, His love and His care.

Chapter 10

Seventeen years had passed. I looked outside and saw several people in a service utility vehicle taking pictures of our home. I went out to see who these people were. To my pleasant surprise, it was the family that we bought the house from. They congratulated me on the outstanding way that we kept the house and landscape looking so beautiful. I believe when God gives us something, we should show appreciation by taking care of it. I also thought about the fact that they bought the house to operate a clinic, but was denied the opportunity by the neighbors, and to think years after, God had it in His plan for me to operate a daycare on the same premises for eleven years.

After the passing of my husband and after the children had branched out on their own, I decided to open a licensed Daycare in my home. It was somewhat tedious at first, but with that entrepreneurial adrenaline flowing I moved on in full force. It was a slow start at first; but with families and friends telling each other about the good care that their children were getting, I started getting other children from the same family.

Things went well, and I started looking around for a larger facility. I saw an advertisement for an established Daycare not far from where I lived. I went and looked at the building and it seemed fine; and it was in a nice area. I contacted the real estate agent who asked that I put down a good faith deposit and sign some papers. When I was asked for additional money, I contacted my attorney who informed me not to sign any more documents until he reviewed them. With my attorney now involved, I felt safe. Later, two more men entered the deal, plus one on the phone who I never met. I was told that I qualified for the purchase of the Daycare building and the business, and they requested an additional amount of money; which I paid. I started feeling that something was not right, and it got worse when I told them I do not want their existing Daycare name. I wanted to use the name that I already had. I wrote to the licensing department requesting that I transfer my current Daycare's name to this new facility. All involved were dead set on me not changing the name of the business that I had planned on buying.

One week before the closing, one of the agents came to my home and announced in a mocking way that I had better be at the closing because my house and in-home Daycare rest on the signing of the documents. I saw that I was taken. I called my attorney asking that he represent me at the closing. He informed me that he was not a real estate attorney and a real estate attorney is what I needed. I felt as if the world was on my shoulders just pressing the life out of me. I was praying, but I felt so alone as if the Lord was not there. I realize how

David felt in Psalm 10:1-3, "*Why stands thou afar off O Lord? Why hides thou thyself in times of trouble?*

The wicked in his pride doth persecute the poor: Let them be taken in the devices that they have imagined.

For the wicked boasted of his heart's desire and blessed the covetous, whom the Lord abhorreth."

Looking at these tall men and me; a poor little widow, I felt like David looking up at Goliath. But I decided it's not time to give up or give in. I needed a good attorney, and I needed him or her right now. I was given the name of an attorney who I immediately contacted. I was relieved to know that he would meet with me on such short notice. I went to his office and before entering the building, I had a premonition to look at the car that pulled up in the parking lot. I could not believe my eyes, it was one of the three men who were making my life a nightmare.

I met with the attorney only to be told that he could not represent me, because the real estate agents that I was dealing with, uses his office for closings on their business dealings. I could not believe this was happening. There was just two more days before the closing of the Daycare deal. In desperation I prayed, "Lord Jesus please. If you never get me out of another dilemma, I am asking you to get me out of this one."

A few hours after I got home, the same agent I saw in the parking lot came to my home and said to me, "Your lawyer has divorced you." It was evident that after I left the lawyer's office, they had discussed the case. Another dagger was stuck in my heart with the intention of trying to get me in a weaker condition.

In desperation, I called my insurance agent and explained the situation. He recommended a lawyer who could meet with me immediately. I walked into the building where the lawyer's office was located with fear trying to get the better of me. I thought to myself; with the size of this office, Lord, how much is he going to charge me? Putting those thoughts aside, I poured out my grief to the lawyer. It's as if everything that was bottled up all these weeks, and all the tears just kept flowing like a river. With two days to go, he went to work immediately. His findings showed that the Daycare building was overpriced and the interest rate was too high. Since I did not think I could get out of this deal; which I would have preferred, I asked that the lawyer review the documents and represent me at the closing.

One day before the closing, I received a call from my lawyer telling me that the closing was off. I asked him to repeat the statement, and he again said, "The closing is off." I thought it was just temporarily postponed and the best was yet to come. He informed me that the sale of the Daycare and building is off, since the agents and Daycare owner tried to sell the business with money owing on it; which is illegal. The lawyer could get back some of the money that I had paid on the deal. God had come through in such a way that it was above and beyond what I had expected. When I realize what these wicked people tried to do to me, I could remember telling the Lord, "If you do not answer another prayer for me; please I beg of you, answer this one." I went to meet this woman that owned the day care that I intended to buy. I tried to look her in the eye to find out her reason for trying to play such a low-down trick on me. I could not get an eye contact from her, but I left her with these words, "The Lord has bottled up tears; "that was the only words I could seem to say to her at that time. I do not know if it's because I was having so many crying spells. 'GOD HAD COME THROUGH FOR ME BEYOND MY WILDEST IMAGINATIONS,' but I was left so tired and weary; crying a lot for a long time. It has been said, 'If the Lord did not think we could handle the situations that he takes us through, he would not have taken us there.'

Reflecting on this situation, I can see the blessing it has brought me. It has left me stronger, wiser and being able to warn people of the pitfalls before it overtakes them. Also for those of us who are novice, finding out the hard way that one of the first thing to do is speak to an attorney before any papers are signed. Not just any attorney, but the attorney for the type of business that you are going into. My reason for saying this is; that when I found out the desperate situation I was in, I asked my attorney who was advising me on the buying of the day care. I will admit, I had signed a paper before I sought his advice. He looked at the paper; he did not sound an alarm, but just told me not to sign anymore papers until I forwarded them to him so that he can look them over. I felt quite safe after that information. When this entire nightmare came about, I asked the attorney to represent me at the closing. This was when I got the last dagger in my heart at the last minute! He informed me that he was not a real estate attorney, and that was who I needed; which left me scrambling at the last minute to get the right person. It also pointed out the importance of getting the business incorporated.

The trials that we go through may not seem to make sense at the time, but God has got it all in control; in due time, he makes it work for his purpose.

When I decided to write this book, I told one of my daughters of my decision to mention some of the achievements and obstacles that some of the children went through; which would include her. Being the kind, thoughtful, calm and considerate person that she was her reply was, "Unless you are going to write about all six children, do not single out anyone." I thought to myself, 'Here was the wisdom of Solomon.' Writing a book about my six children, I imagine would be a best seller. From playing tricks on the lady we hired to help with the housework, to the sibling rivalry. Just thinking about one incident, where I was busy in the kitchen and the house that was always noisy and then went dead silent. Instantly I said to myself, 'This is not good.' I went around the house calling their names; there was absolutely no answer. Finally, I looked in our bedroom under the bed, and there were all six children lying on their stomachs. My youngest son; who is the fifth child, with the gun in his hand pointing as if they are waiting in ambush. If I was not lying on the floor looking for them at the time, I may have fainted. This was a gun that I had asked my husband not to purchase, but he insisted that it is for protecting the family and would be locked away. Thinking of all the mishaps that have happened with children; like getting their hands on a gun that were supposed to be locked away in a safe place, it just made me more appreciative of God's goodness and His protection to us.

Jamaica is the third largest Island in the Caribbean. Spain held the Island against the Buccaneer raids at the main city at the time which is called Spanish Town. England claimed the Island in a raid, but the Spanish did not relinquish their claim to the Island until 1670. Over the years Jamaica went through many uprising from outside; including piracy. In 1938, the People's National Party (PNP) was founded. Its main rival was the Jamaican Labor Party (JLP) which was established in 1942. The first election between both parties was held under universal suffrage in 1944. The first Prime Minister was Alexander Bustamante of the JLP. In 1962 under the leadership of Prime Minister Michael Manley, Jamaica won its independence from England. With the Island already fraying at its edges, things got worse. There were so many illegal guns on the streets; people were being killed and there was fighting between rival gangs. The Prime Minister sent out a mandatory call for all guns to be turned into the Police or face indefinite detention with no trial.

There were times in our marriage that my husband and I did not see things eye to eye, but somehow we could iron out our differences. When we got married, my father-in-law had a long hunting gun which was handed down to him. My husband was determined that his guns stayed in his house. The more I thought about it, the more I was convinced that I needed to do something. I took the long hunting gun, wrapped it up carefully and got on the bus to the Halfway Tree Police Station in St. Andrew. There I handed the gun over to the police and got a receipt for it. When my husband came home from work, I told him what I had done. It did not set well with him, but I was totally convinced in my heart that I did the right thing. I would not recommend this solution to everyone, unless you know how far you can go in your relationship with each other. The call kept going out for everyone to turn their guns in. My husband decided that there is no way they are going to make him turn the revolver in, because it's for the protection of his family.

Shortly thereafter, a police came to our home and questioned my husband asking if he had any guns in the house. He told the police yes. He was taken down to the Police Station with the gun. No one who was taken in for disobeying the Prime Minister was to be released. This was when the steps that I had taken came into consideration. Had I not turn that gun in, the results would have been devastating. He would have been locked up without a trial like the others. He was released, because they found where the other gun was turned in. Had it not been turned in; he would have been disobeying the law by hiding his guns. Thank God for my insight and wisdom. I think we should be there for each other when either of our thinking is off track and not be too stubborn to admit it.

I do not consider myself as someone who procrastinates; but in writing this book, there was a long pause. During that time, I remember one of my sons approached me and abruptly asked, "Mom, what about that book that you were writing?" My mind went back to the times that I told my children, "To be successful, you must be consistent. What-so-ever you start, finish it. Don't be a quitter." Therefore, I must finish what I started. This was also confirmed when a minister visited our congregation. He asked the audience about the many things that we had started and never finished; like the book that you started and never finished? That was my final wake up call.

Being a member of a church is being a member of the body of Christ. When one has a concern; especially when that person voices the concern more than once directly to me, I thought it was time to address the subject. Upon investigating the situation, I realized that someone was needed to assist an elderly gentleman.   I offered to go by for a few hours just to read or converse with the individual.   I had retired and loved it; especially, since I no longer had to listen to the alarm clock anymore.

I finally met the elderly gentleman.   He was an educator by profession, very disciplined in certain areas, loved the outdoors with a passion and was eager to have interesting and informative conversations.   I was fascinated and impressed by the amount and variety of tropical fruit trees and other types of plants that he had planted over the years. The amazing thing is; that the land space was not a vast amount of space, but it was utilized wisely.   These are some of the plants that were included his collection: mangoes, avocados, cherries, guavas, grapes, bananas, ackees; the national fruit of Jamaica. This fruit must be cooked before it is eaten. Ackee was brought to Jamaica from Africa and was later introduced to Haiti, Cuba,

Barbados and later Florida. He also had citrus: such as limes; and at one time, some of the sweetest grapefruits. There were also tubers: such as cassava and yams also vegetables. The gentleman explained that he planted them in cycles that throughout the year there is something fresh on the table. Every day if the weather permits, he would be outside inspecting the trees for the appearance of the first buds. He can predict every progress until they get to the table.

I went there to spend a few hours, but I ended up been asked to fill in for a week. There was such a drastic change in his eating habits and his outlook on life. And most importantly; since over the years he was in the habit of dressing in his suit and tie for work and church, there wasn't any problem getting ready for church. And if someone decides to get his suit, tie and shoes together, that person better be sure he or she knows how to coordinate well.

I was asked to come to come back and fill in for another two weeks; I ended up helping for over two years. There were challenging times; the experiences that I gained from listening to his words of wisdom, watching those buds and blossoms appear, watching them mature until they got to the table and most of all having the joy of helping to lift someone's spirit. Seeing a smile where there was none, makes it all worthwhile. I was brought into this situation in an unusual way, but I think it was all in God's plan. I would take care of that man as if I was taking care of my own father. After being there for over two years, I had to start thinking of my own health; I had to reluctantly say goodbye. He passed away shortly after; which I was sorry to hear, but glad I had been a part of his life.

Proverbs 31:10-12, *"Who can find a virtuous woman? For her price is above rubies. The heart of her husband doth safely trust in her so that he shall have no need of spoil. She shall do him good and not evil all the days of her life."*

There are times when circumstances arise in our lives that leave us devastated and financially challenged. This was one of my big moments. I had myself a pity party asking the Lord, 'Why?' Then I decided, I had to apply for a loan to take care of this debt. Without telling anyone of my situation, I applied for the loan. 'But God," when he has our back, we are fully covered. Unexpectedly, money started coming in from all angles. My former employer, who I did not just give eye service to; Colossians 3:22, but gave a fair days' work for a fair days' pay. When I resigned from that employment, my new employer called to get a work reference. They told me that your former employer described you as a gem. This had to do with my upbringing, but most of all the Lord being in my life.

As a child, I could not understand why my parents kept giving when we needed it. It is amazing how I ended up walking in the same footsteps. They were doing what the Lord said in Ecclesiastes 11:1-2, *"Cast thy bread upon the waters: for thou shall find it after many days. Give a portion to seven and to eight: for thou know not what evil shall be upon the earth, (i.e.)."* Give freely, cast it; though it may seem thrown away, it will not sink. Send it as a voyage, you shall receive a harvest. Verse 2:-Keep giving.

This book would not be complete, without writing about the very daughter who I consulted. I am sure her other siblings would not object to this, because of the situations she faced and is still facing. They all wonder about her strength and courage. In one of her sister's own words she said, "If it was me going through all that sickness and pain, I would just roll over and die." This daughter; the third of six children, was diagnosed with Lupus. I had never heard of Lupus before that diagnosis. After finding out more about the disease, I was shaken up. Her illness did not hold her back. Her research enabled her to find out quite a lot about the disease and how it affects the body. She attended seminars about lupus and was later speaking at seminars. She worked as a Paralegal during all of it and volunteered as a Court Appointed Special Advocate for children in the court system. In no way, does my daughter let this disease control her life. I hope and pray that before long, a cure will be found for this terrible disease.

I dedicate this section to the men and women; including my son, who served and are serving this country of ours; The United States of America. I salute them for their unselfish dedication to keeping us safe. I had the opportunity to visit some of them in person while attending my son's retirement from the Navy. One of the things that stood out in my mind was how young some of them were. They were very sad to see my son who was their Chief is retiring. Reflecting back, I remember how my son had that same youthful look when he left home over twenty-three years ago; when he joined the Navy. My appreciation and prayers go out to all the men and women who work so hard to keep us safe. Also to their families, who sacrifice in different ways, in the absence of their loved ones being so far away from home.

There are different situations that we face in life. Sometimes it takes us down in the valley and other times up the mountain. And sometimes it seems as if everything is at a complete standstill. But we need to keep looking to the hills from whence cometh our help; knowing that our help cometh from the Lord, which made heaven and earth.

God wants us to have stability in our lives; not be tossed to and fro. He either sends us to the jeweler's shop to be melted in the fire, molded and made into beautiful jewelry, or plants us in the forest for one hundred years that we may grow up to be a giant oak tree.

161

Great souls mature through storms and struggles. It does not feel good at the time, but looking back with amazement; it makes us feel so much stronger. It helps us to be able to grow in grace and can encourage others.

I hope by reading this book, you are more determined to face the obstacles that are thrown in your pathway; knowing that the Lord can keep you from falling. Casting all your cares upon him; for He careth for you.

Proverbs 18:10 tell us that, "*the name of the Lord is strong tower: The righteous runneth into it and is safe.*"

Isaiah 12: 4, "*And in that day, shall ye say, Praise the Lord, call upon his name declare is name among the people, make mention that his name is exalted.*"

Philippians 2:9, *"Wherefore God also hath highly exalted him, and given him a name which is above every name."*

St. John 14:14, *"If ye shall ask anything in my name, I will do it. I have proven this over and over in my life."*

Knowing the importance of the 'Names of the Lord Jesus' in our spiritual walk with Him, will help us to know Him more intimately, experience His sufficiency, his majesty, His awesome power and His expressed commitment to us.

Jehovah-Jire	Our Provider	Genesis 22:14
Jehovah-Nissi	Our banner	Exodus 17:15
Jehovah-Shammah	The Lord is there	Exodus 48:35
Jehovah-Shalom	Our Peace	Judges 6:24

Jehovah-Ro'Eh	Our Shepherd	Psalm 23:1
Jehovah-Tsidkenu	Our righteousness	Jeremiah 23:56
Jehovah-Rapha	Our Healer	Exodus 15:26
Elohim	Faithful and true God	Revelation 19:11
El Elyou	Most high God	Psalm 47:2
El Shaddai	All sufficient God	Jeremiah 32:17
Adonai	Our Lord and Master	Psalm 24:1